1 MONTH OF
FREE
READING

at

www.ForgottenBooks.com

By purchasing this book you are eligible for one month membership to ForgottenBooks.com, giving you unlimited access to our entire collection of over 1,000,000 titles via our web site and mobile apps.

To claim your free month visit:

www.forgottenbooks.com/free202473

ISBN 978-0-483-68494-2
PIBN 10202473

This book is a reproduction of an important historical work. Forgotten Books uses
state-of-the-art technology to digitally reconstruct the work, preserving the original format
whilst repairing imperfections present in the aged copy. In rare cases, an imperfection in
the original, such as a blemish or missing page, may be replicated in our edition. We do,
however, repair the vast majority of imperfections successfully; any imperfections that
remain are intentionally left to preserve the state of such historical works.

REV.ᴅ BERNARD WHITMAN.

Pub.ᵈ by Benj.ⁿ H Greene

MEMOIR

OF THE

Rev. BERNARD WHITMAN.

BY JASON WHITMAN.

BOSTON:

BENJAMIN H. GREENE.

1837.

CM

Tuttle, Weeks & Dennett....Power Press....17, School Street.

PREFACE.

It was with extreme reluctance that the writer undertook to prepare the following sketch of a beloved and lamented brother; — knowing how apt the public are to attribute all that may be said under such circumstances to feelings of family partiality, and believing that there were others better qualified than himself for the task. The task was declined by others and urged upon the writer. Believing that the true character of the Rev. Bernard Whitman was not known to those who judged only by his published writings, and that if properly set forth it was calculated to do good, by shewing the power of individual energy and the value of personal piety, he has at last made the attempt.

The principles which have guided him in the performance of his task, have been, to exbibit distinctly the materials out of which, and the influences under which the character was formed, and then to set forth the character itself just as it was. He has availed himself, as far as he has been able, of the kindness of friends, because he thought that testimony from others would be more acceptable and would have more weight than what he might himself write. To those friends of whose kindness he has availed himself he would tender his most sincere thanks.

The publication of the work has been delayed in consequence of the multiplicity of cares and labors resulting from the peculiar situations in which the writer has been placed; having been for a time after the decease of his brother engaged in the duties of a public and travelling agency, and afterwards in ministering to a new but rapidly increasing religious society. It is now given to the public in the hope and with the prayer that it may aid in the promotion of the best interests of truth and piety — interests to which the subject of the sketch was devoted while among us, and in the promotion of which he sacrificed his health and life.

JASON WHITMAN.

Portland, Me.

CONTENTS.

CHAPTER IV.

MEMOIR

OF THE

REV. BERNARD WHITMAN.

MEMOIR.

CHAPTER I.

Birth — Features of mind and character in early life — Father's character — Mother's character — Mode of family government — Father's pecuniary circumstances — Common town school — Religious impressions — Leaves the paternal roof, to work in a cotton manufactory — Commences study.

BERNARD WHITMAN, the subject of this memoir, was born at East Bridgewater, Mass., June 8th, 1796. He was the son of Deacon John Whitman by a second wife — the thirteenth child of his father, the eleventh of his mother. From birth he was a hearty and robust child, blessed with an apparently good constitution, and enjoyed almost uninterrupted health. His character was, from the first, strongly marked. The features of his mind, manifested in early years, were the same by which he was distinguished in after life. They were amiableness and generosity of disposition, an open frankness of manner, ardor, activity and perseverance in the

2

pursuit of the various objects of desire, and fearlessness in regard to personal danger. To these
were added, as his mind began to develope itself
more fully, an abhorrence of all that was mean,
underhanded or deceitful, a love of justice, and
a resolute boldness in its assertion and defence.
These characteristics secured for him the love
of his schoolmates, and the deep interest of all
who knew him. His ardor, perseverance and
fearlessness placed him at the head of his school-
mates in all enterprises of difficulty or danger;
not that he was ambitious of this distinction,
but because the post was voluntarily assigned to
him by those less active and fearless than himself. An anecdote may illustrate this. The
boys of the school were one day at play in a pine
grove near the school-house. A hornet's nest
was discovered. This at once interrupted the
play, and excited the desire for its destruction.
A consultation was held, and the plan was laid.
It was to prepare a plug, and insert it into the
only aperture which these insects leave as the
entrance to their dwelling, and then to destroy
the nest with its inmates in such a manner as might
seem best. But when the plan was laid, the ardor
of most began to cool; they were unwilling to
expose themselves to danger in its execution.
Whitman was called upon, and, without hesitation,

he prepared and inserted the plug, and bore off the obnoxious nest in triumph. Those who have known the subject of this memoir during the latter part of his life, will perceive that this is in perfect keeping with his whole character; for they will remember that in manhood, whenever he was convinced that the cause of truth and piety demanded the effort, he was ready to march boldly up to any class of opposers, regardless of the odium to which he might himself be exposed, and utterly indifferent as to the buz which might be raised about his ears, or the stings which might be aimed at his character.

During his childhood the church in East Bridgewater, of which his father was a deacon, was for some time destitute of a pastor. Several of the young gentlemen who supplied the pulpit as candidates, boarded with Deacon Whitman. These all became deeply interested in Bernard, and took much notice of him. One in particular, a Mr Hall, who was fond of children, and who had a happy faculty of winning their affections, spent much time in talking with him about going to college and becoming a minister. It is difficult to trace the secret influences which operate upon the mind of a child, and to assign to each its appropriate share in the formation of the character of the man. But it is supposed that the course pursued by the subject of this memoir, in after life, was much influenced, if not wholly determined, by the deep impressions made thus early upon his mind in these conver-sations; for his was not a mind from which im-pressions once made were easily effaced. Nor was he one who would readily give up the pur-suit of an object on which his affections had once been placed. One circumstance would seem to indicate that he was influenced by strong early impressions. Upon his arrival at the age when most, from their haste to be men engaged in the active business of life, waver much in their plans and purposes, there was, no wavering with him. He formed his resolution without consultation or advice, with many and great obstacles in full view before him, and with a perfect knowledge that the course he marked out would much re-tard his entrance upon the active duties of life. He resolved, under these circumstances, to acquire a collegiate education, and to devote himself to the work of the Christian ministry. In confirmation of these statements in regard to the characteristic features of his early life, an extract from a letter, written by one who boarded for a time in the family of his father, and who was for several years the pastor of the church in

East Bridgewater, is here inserted: — "I have very distinct impressions of his manly form, and of his leading traits of character, when a boy of thirteen or fourteen years; and, as is usual in strongly marked characters, these traits more and more developed, and acquiring a bolder relief by time, accompanied him through his active and useful life. I then saw in Bernard, the boy, the same openness, fearlessness, activity, resolution, perseverance, love of truth, and generous disdain of deceit, of wrong and of oppression, together with the same promptness and zeal to assert and maintain the just rights and lawful claims of others, as well as his own, which were afterwards so conspicuous in the man — the enlightened, sincere and warm-hearted Christian — the devout and indefatigable minister."

To understand fully the development of mind and the growth of character, it is important to become acquainted with the influences to which the individual is in early life subjected. · These constitute that incidental education, which is often more powerful in the formation of character than direct instruction. These, in the case before us, were somewhat peculiar. Dea. John Whitman, the father, was a man the peculiar features of whose character were so prominent and striking as to attract notice, and

2*

exert a powerful influence upon all around. In regard to his religious opinions, it may be necessary, in these days of division, to speak with caution. The high-toned Calvinist might have claimed him, and might have rested his claim, and with some degree of plausibility too, upon the fact that he used the Assembly's Catechism in the religious instruction of his children. And then, too, the zealous Arminian of that day might have claimed him, and might have rested his claim, and with good reason, upon the fact that he always associated and acted with the Arminians; that whenever there was a division in any ecclesiastical body of which he was a member, Dea. Whitman was always found on the liberal or Arminian side. The truth is, he never was a party man. He thought much more highly of correctness in life, than of correctness in creed, as evidence that the heart is regenerated by gospel influences. He was, and still is, a decided Trinitarian, in one sense of that term. (He still is — for he is still living, in the enjoyment of good health, and with his mental and bodily powers in a comparatively good degree of vigor, at the advanced age of one hundred and one years.) But whatever might have been the peculiar shades of his own belief upon the doctrine of the Trinity and upon kindred doctrines, they were never brought forward as matters of prominence and importance. They were not the subjects of his inquiries in regard to strangers, nor of his daily conversations before his children. They were not inculcated and dwelt upon as the essentials of religion, without which one could not be regarded as a Christian or a pious man; cousequently, they exerted but little direct and immediate influence upon the religious opinions of his children.

But, if we pass from his religious opinions to his religious and moral character, we find that strongly marked. The most prominent feature of his religious character was an unbending devotion to duty. This was not confined to what are by some regarded as especially religious duties. It was carried out into all the various transactions of every day life. Every one who knew him, felt that he would sooner cut off a right hand than be guilty of what he believed to be a wrong action. He was a man of great, pervading and constantly operating religious sensibility. This religious sensibility consisted not in proneness to physical excitement, but in tenderness of conscience. Religion with him was not mere zeal, discussing, defending and spreading opinions; nor powerful impulse, filling

the soul with thrilling but short-lived emotions;
it was principle, firmly seated in the heart, constantly governing and guiding the life.

There were other traits in close connexion
with this. There was a deep feeling of humility, indicated by his conduct, rather than proclaimed in his words; by his ever taking the
lower seat, rather than by humiliating expressions
in regard to himself. There was a high regard
for the institutions and ordinances of religion,
indicated by his liberality, according to his
means, in the support of the one, and his punctuality in the observance of the other. There
was perfect charity towards those who differed
from him. He claimed the right of judging for
himself, and without any forthputting pretences
to independence of character, he ever, with unwavering firmness, exercised the right which he
claimed. But he was ever willing that others
should do the same. It is doubted whether he
was ever heard to speak unkindly of any one on
account of a difference of opinion upon religious
subjects. He has been heard to lament and rebuke the opposite course in others. He could
unite in prayer, in praise, and in the holy communion of the Lord's supper with those of his
children who were Unitarian in sentiment, with
the same cordiality with which he united with

those who were Trinitarian in opinion. There was manifested in his whole life that gospel charity which hopeth all things; a willingness to make all proper allowances; to hope that motives might be good, and that good results might follow, even where appearances were unfavorable. There was a strong aversion to all extravagant religious excitements. This resulted from his view of a religious life, as consisting in uniform obedience; from his natural evenness of temperament, seldom much excited by passions or emotions; from the regularity of his general habits of living, and from his having witnessed, in early life, practices in connexion with religious excitements, which he regarded as sinful. On this subject he expressed himself decidedly and sometimes in tones of solemn admonition. The following extract from a letter written at the age of ninety, to a son then residing in a place where he had understood religious excitements were prevailing, will manifest his feelings at that time. "I would not have you try to raise your name by doing two days' work in one, but by working well and steadily. I hope you will remember the first day, and attend meeting as steadily as your health and the care of your family will admit, and work the other six. I should not advise you to go to night

meetings, nor to any week day meetings frequently. I trust you will be as much in the way
of your duty, and as much out of the way of
temptation, while about your business, as at any
other place." The union of the several features
which have been noticed, presented a complete
and well balanced religious character. There
was manifested, in every act and circumstance
of life, the true spirit of religion. He seemed
ever to have his eye fixed upon heavenly things;
to walk by faith, and not by sight; to live for
eternity rather than for time. He was diligent
in the labors of his occupation; faithful in the
discharge of all incumbent duties; prudent and
economical in his expenses; for he felt that he
was ever under the inspection of an omniscient
eye — ever accountable to God. But never did
he speak of, or seem to regard wealth as worthy
to become the object of man's greatest anxieties
and most strenuous labors. Never did he speak
of, or seem to regard those who were amassing
wealth simply, as the persons who were doing
well in the world. The moral and religious
character were regarded by him as far more important than all outward and earthly enjoyments,
possessions and distinctions. Where the purity
of these was endangered by exposure to temptation and sin, he trembled for the individual, how

great soever might be his worldly prosperity.
Where circumstances were favorable to the
purity and proper growth of these, he felt satisfied, even though the individual might be exposed to poverty, or subjected to affliction.
Amid all the varying scenes of life he was
cheerful, for he cherished an unwavering trust
and confidence in the goodness of God, and in
the wisdom of all the allotments of his providence. He had learned in whatever state he
was, to be contented. Such was the religious
character of the father of the subject of this
memoir.

In this connexion may be mentioned a striking
trait of moral and social virtue. It was a singular and uniform devotion to the cause of
temperance. At a time when all around him
regarded the daily use of ardent spirit as bene-
ficial, at least, if not absolutely necessary, Dea.
Whitman abstained. He kept the article, it is
true, in his house, not as a drink, but as medi-
cine. Nor did he confine himself on this subject to his own practices, or the regulation of
his own household. So great did the evils of intemperance appear to him to be, so insidious and
imperceptible its approaches, that he felt it to be
a duty to speak openly and decidedly upon the
subject to his friends and neighbors. Never

did he suffer a friend to retail the dangerous article without a remonstrance, or repeated remonstrances from him.

It is not to be supposed that a man of Deacon Whitman's character would be indifferent to the education of his children. He was extremely solicitous on this point; not, indeed, in regard to the particular branches they might study, nor the amount of learning they might acquire; but in regard to the right direction of their minds, and the proper formation of their characters. He was anxious not that they might be distinguished for genius or learning, but that they might fear God, and endeavor to be useful to men.

The mother of the subject of this memoir was a perfect counterpart to her husband, coinciding with him in all his views and feelings. Or, if she differed from him at all, it was in the possession of a more ardent and sanguine temperament; in looking, if not more uniformly, at least with a more intense gaze, upon the bright side of things. She fully and zealously co-operated with her husband in efforts for the moral and religious improvement of their children, and by her energy, perseverance, and cheerful trust in Providence, greatly aided him in his endeavors. Bernard is thought to have inherited the temperament of his mother, and to have manifested a strong resemblance to her in the peculiar features of his mind and character.

In the family government to which Bernard, together with his brothers and sisters, were subjected, there was much of uniformity, firmness and decision, but nothing of severity. The influence exerted was that of example, rather than that of precept; that of regular training, rather than that of occasional excitement. There was addressed to the children but very little direct and solemn exhortation to become religious. But there were continually before them living representations of the beauty and happiness of a religious life. Instruction was conveyed, right feelings cherished, and proper principles implanted, by means of anecdotes and incidental conversations. In this way, ideas like the following were continually thrown out — that we should be ever on our guard against the inventions of men in matters of religion; that we should ever be satisfied with the allotments of Providence; that every one should feel it to be a duty to attend meeting twice on the Sabbath, when not necessarily detained; that if possible, they should attend upon the preaching of one of their own sentiments; but if not, they should still attend, for a well disposed mind could de-

rive profit from the preaching of any good man,
to whatever denomination he might belong; that
the multiplication of religious services was often
a device of the devil, to drive out one good thing
with another; that expressions of peace and joy
at the approach of death were gratifying to
friends, but were no sure evidence that the
heart is right with God; that the evidence of this
is to be sought in obedience of life; that one
should not adopt the religious opinions of another
because they are opinions of that other, even
though he might be a father or a religious
teacher, but should adopt only such as might,
after careful examination, approve themselves to
his own mind; that one should never sneer at,
or ridicule the religious observances of others;
that a person unable to dispense with the daily
use of ardent spirit, had already become en-
slaved, and was in great danger of being ruined.
These, and a vast variety of similar ideas, were
the subjects, not of direct addresses and appeals,
and protracted conversations, but of apparently
casual remarks. An anecdote would be related,
or an incidental observation made, or a maxim
stated, not with the apparent purpose of instructing the children, but simply as called forth
by the ever varying circumstances of domestic
life. In this way, these ideas became familiar

to the minds of the children, and characterized
the social and moral atmosphere which they
were continually breathing. When any of the
children were about to leave the paternal roof,
or enter upon any new and important relation in
life, there was no long, formal, common-place
advice; there was only some short and simple
but pithy maxim or direction. When the subject of this memoir, for example, was about to
enter upon the duties of the ministerial office,
there was given by the father only this simple
but important direction, *"Seek for truth, and
follow duty."* Such was the general tone and
spirit of Dea. Whitman's family government.
In perfect consistency with this spirit were his
regularity in family devotions, and his great
punctuality in attendance upon the public worship of the sanctuary. Never did a day pass
without the assembling together of the family,
the devout reading of the scriptures, and the
fervent prayer, both at morning and at evening.
Never was there a meal partaken of without the
humble supplication of a blessing at its commencement, and the joyful return of thanks at
its close. Never did a Sabbath pass without
assembling as many of the family as could be
assembled, at the house of worship. The peculiarity of this family government consisted in

this, that the parents endeavored to govern themselves as well as their children. They manifested their deep regard for religion, not by continually talking to their children upon the subject, but by quietly and perseveringly maintaining before them a truly christian spirit and deportment, by leading in their presence truly religious lives. The peculiar character of the parents and of their mode of family government exerted the happiest influence upon the subject of this memoir, in tempering, guiding and restraining his natural propensities, in implanting correct principles and forming virtuous habits, in laying the foundation for precisely the cast of character which he afterwards exhibited.

But there are other circumstances in the early life of Mr Whitman which are thought to have exerted a powerful influence upon his subsequent character. His father, although raised above absolute want, was never possessed of wealth. With a family of fourteen children, it was often difficult, and at times absolutely impossible to make the expenditures and the receipts of the year correspond. The children were, cousequently, early called upon to put forth their own exertions. They frequently worked for the neighbors, that so they might assist their father or procure something for themselves. Whatever of pocket money they had, was the result of their own exertions. They raised and sold eggs and poultry, they were allowed to possess each a sheep or two, that by the sale of the lambs or the fleece they might add to their store. They followed the rivers and scoured the woods. The musk-rat, the woodchuck, the rabbit and the partridge, were the objects of their search and the sources of their gain. In these pursuits Bernard was peculiarly active, energetic and persevering. In this way the natural features of his mind were strengthened and developed, and his character became more and more strongly marked. There was manifested thus early, a spirit of enterprise, a feeling of independence in regard to others, and a confidence in his powers, seldom seen in one so young. Undoubtedly, much of the unconquerable energy of his subsequent character is to be attributed to the straitened circumstances of his early years, by which he was compelled to put forth strenuous exertions, to exercise much contrivance and forethought and judgment, to rely solely upon himself with the feeling that if, in any of his plans, he should fail of success, he had no one to whom he could look for support, and no inherited wealth on which to repose in ease and comfort.

3*

Then, too, the advantages of early education enjoyed by Mr Whitman were only those afforded by a common town school. And, after the age of ten or twelve, he attended even this school only three months during the winter, and worked upon the farm during the remainder of the year. This circumstance was not without its peculiar influence. He was accustomed during his early years to regard active and useful labor as the appropriate business of life, and to consider study, books, knowledge of all kinds, but as the means of more extensive usefulness. He had ever heard a good education spoken of by his parents as one of the most valuable bequests which can be bestowed upon children, far more valuable than all gold and silver. But, in the same connexion, perhaps in the same breath, he had heard it spoken of as valuable only because it might be the means of more extensive usefulness. And this was the light in which he ever regarded reading, books, study. He was fond of reading, he was willing to study hard, he did actually acquire an extensive acquaintance with books. But he ever regarded these as valuable, not so much in themselves considered, as because they might render him more extensively useful in the profession of his choice. It was a remark which he frequently made, that we have but a short time in which to work, that there is much to be done in removing error and sin, and establishing truth and holiness, that it is wrong, therefore, to waste our time upon books and in study which will afford us no assistance in the accomplishment of the most important work of life. In accordance with this remark, he endeavored to make all his own reading bear, more or less directly, upon the labors in which he was engaged.

Still further, at the common town school he mingled freely with children of his own standing in society, the children of the common people. All the modes of thinking and reasoning and speaking prevalent among the people were perfectly familiar to him. They were his own modes of thinking, reasoning and speaking. He never, it is true, become that accurate scholar in all the minutiæ of learning, which he might have been, had his attention been directed to study from his earliest years, and his time passed among books and in literary society. But in the place of this he had acquired an intimate knowledge of the human mind, as manifested among the great mass of the people, and as developed in the ordinary circumstances of life. He knew how to approach the mind under these circumstances so as to secure the attention, and lead the thoughts to the conclusions he desired to establish. He had not looked upon the great mass of the people from an elevated or a retired place of observation. He had been with them, he was himself one of them, born in their midst and trained up in their midst; consequently, he ever deeply sympathised with them in all their trials and difficulties, in all their feelings and wishes. These circumstances of his early life gave a peculiarity to his knowledge of human nature. He had not studied human nature more thoroughly than the closeted philosopher, nor did he understand it better. He could not probably have described it in the abstract so well. But then he knew better how to apply his knowledge of human nature in his intercourse with his fellow men. He regarded this, like all other knowledge, but as an instrument of usefulness, and it was his strongest desire so to make use of every means of influence in his power, as to subserve the interests of humanity, and promote the glory of God in the spread of truth and the increase of piety.

The features of mind manifested by Mr Whitman in early childhood, the circumstances of his early life, the character of his parents, and the peculiar mode of their family government, have been dwelt upon and developed simply for the purpose of showing the materials of which his character was made, and the influences under which it was formed.

Until the age of sixteen, Bernard spent his time with his father, in the manner which has been mentioned, attending school in the winter and working upon the farm in the summer. His religious impressions at this period related to duty rather than to religious feelings. The character of his parents, and the peculiar circumstances in which he was placed, were such as were calculated to fill him with the deepest reverence for the christian character, to form him to habits of religious obedience, and to excite within him great tenderness of conscience in regard to duty, but they were no less calculated to suppress all free conversation upon the subject of religious feelings. The parents were not accustomed to watch carefully every variation of these and to speak of them as of importance. The children then could not be expected to do this. There is the best of all possible evidence, that afforded by his conduct, that there was beginning to prevail within him an inviolable regard for duty, that he abhorred a wrong action, that correct principles were beginning to take root, and that virtuous habits were in the process of formation. Some of his conversations, too, with the writer of this, are remembered, conversations upon the discourses heard on the Sabbath. These consisted, not in minute criticism, nor in general censure or applause, but in particular practical self-application. These circumstances are mentioned to show that the foundation of a religious character was laid, even in youth, in deep and rightly directed reverence, in great tenderness of conscience, and in habitual obedience to the will of God as made known in the gospel of his Son ; that he had formed those habits of thought and reflection upon the subject of religion, and was in the practice of applying to himself the religious instruction with which he might be favored, which indicate deep personal interest in the subject, and often lead to entire self-devotion to the cause of the Redeemer.

About the age of sixteen, Bernard made known his wishes, or rather his determination to acquire a public education. He had no hopes of pecnniary assistance from his father. But he received what was considered as equivalent, his time from the age of sixteen until he should be legally his own master at the age of twentyone. It was his plan to earn the sum of one hundred dollars, and then to commence his studies. He sought, therefore, for that employment in which this sum could be most easily and expeditiously earned. He at length found employment in a cotton manufactory, at Mansfield, Mass., of which an older brother was at that time overseer; where he spent one year as an apprentice, in making himself acquainted with the business. He was then employed and received wages. His employer speaks of him at this period of his life as "one who was esteemed a faithful and trusty hand, and who maintained an unblemished character." From Mansfield he removed to Hansen, Mass., where he spent a few months. He then returned to Mansfield, where he became the principal overseer in a new and different manufactory from that in which he had before worked. Here he remained until he had secured his hundred dollars and was prepared, according to his original plan, to commence his studies. He now returned to his father's house and attended the academy in Bridgewater, about two miles distant, that he might enjoy the advantages of regular instruction in this the commencement of his studies.

CHAPTER II.

In September, 1816, Mr Whitman entered the Academy at Exeter, N. H., and was for two years under the instruction of that much beloved and eminently successful teacher of youth, Benjamin Abbott, LL. D. He was received into the institution as a beneficiary, supported from the Phillips charity fund. The peculiarities of his character so far as they were developed while here may be learned from the testimony of his instructer. — "It cannot be expected," he says, "in ordinary cases, after the lapse of nearly twenty years, in the succession of numbers, that very vivid impressions of each indi-

vidual will be left on the mind. Your brother,
however, in some measure forms an exception
to this remark. I well remember that ardor of
mind, strength of resolution, and benevolent
activity, were then prominent traits of his character. There was, at that time, a military company composed of the students of the Academy,
formed by the present Secretary of War while
a member of the institution, and still continued
with considerable reputation. Exercises of the
kind were then thought a salutary relaxation for
the studious and sedentary, and a substitute for
amusements less innocent and manly. Your
brother entered spiritedly into these exercises,
and was principally instrumental in forming a
second company, from a smaller class of boys,
as an appendage to the first. Over both of these
he exercised almost unbounded control. The
exertions necessary to regulate and control such
a variety of dispositions, as must be found in
such an assemblage of youth voluntarily assembled for purposes of amusement, required no
ordinary share of popular talents and probably
not a little time and thought, which might otherwise have been devoted to the minuter and
more difficult parts of classic studies. How
much these exercises might engross his feelings
and intrench upon the time and perseverance

necessary to form the thoroughly accurate scholar, cannot now be readily decided. I would not be understood to suggest that his scholarship was inferior. It certainly was not, but it was less distinguished than it would have been with the whole force of his ardent mind directed exclusively to objects purely classic and literary. I mention these facts, because they had undoubtedly a bearing upon his standing as a scholar at the time, and an influence on his character in after life, which has been so distinguished for benevolent activity, and successful exertion in the cause of human improvement."

In connexion with the testimony of his instructer, may be given some extracts from a letter written by one, who was his school fellow while at Exeter, and his classmate in College, relating to the same period of his life. " Being several years his junior, I did not enjoy that peculiar sort of intimacy with him, which would furnish materials such as you desire. Any attempt of mine to delineate the honest, straight forward energy of his character, the warmth of his friendship, or the untiring zeal with which he sought after what be deemed to be *useful* in his literary course, would be but a faint repetition of what you have probably before this received from others nearer his standing in point of years. An incident occurs to me which, although trifling in itself, forcibly illustrates that principle of active benevolence which marked his character through life. When a student at the Academy, the good lady with whom he boarded requested him, one cold stormy winter's morning, to ascertain the situation of two poor old women, who lived in a neighboring garret. They were a mother and daughter, the mother ninetyeight, and the daughter between seventy and eighty years of age. The picture of shivering misery they presented affected him so strongly, that, when he came to school he was totally unfit for his usual duties. We occupied the same desk, and I soon found out the cause of his distress. A subscription paper was drawn up, and, though his purse was at that time rather light, he contributed more in accordance with his feelings than his ability. I was to translate Cicero for him, while he was to perform the more active duties of charity for the rest of us. A stock of fuel was soon purchased and a man hired to saw it. The money was expended and the wood was yet to be carried up stairs, which the man refused to do without further compensation. The charitable feelings of the rest of us were satisfied when our money was paid. But he, without asking the assistance of any

one, secretly labored the whole evening, that so
good a work might be well and completely done;
and returned to his boarding house more happy
with having secured the comfort of these two
poor creatures for the winter, than he would
have been in the possession of thousands."

From the above extracts, it will be seen, that
the peculiarities of mind manifested in early
life were in a process of development while at
the Academy at Exeter. The same features
were more prominent than before, and were
ripening into confirmed traits of character. It
was with him, as it is with many who commence
study late in life. He did not become thoroughly
accurate in all the minutiæ of classic literature.
He had, before commencing his studies, received
an impulse, which urged him on in a course of
energetic and benevolent activity. He had
formed the habit of regarding knowledge as the
means of usefulness. It is presumed that it
was no part of his desire, while acquiring an
education, to become distinguished merely as a
scholar; his desire was, that he might so discipline and train and inform his mind, as to be
useful in his day and generation. In accordance
with this feeling, he was, as we have learned
from his school-mate, untiring in his zeal in the
pursuit of what he *deemed to be useful* in his

literary course. He was, as has been intimated by his teacher, in the minuter and more difficult parts of classic studies, undoubtedly deficient; while at the same time he seized upon and was prepared to apply in practice, the great principles and philosophical truths set forth in the authors studied.

As in his early years, so at the Academy, he was universally esteemed. He is often spoken of by the good lady with whom he boarded, in terms of strong interest, as one who was kind and obliging, easily satisfied, and ever ready to render all the assistance in his power. He was much beloved by the students who were near his own age and standing, while he was regarded by the smaller boys as their champion, the bold asserter and unflinching defender of their rights.

While at Exeter, we find traces of peculiar impressions upon the subject of religion. Indeed, he was prepared, by the influences and education of early life, to lend an attentive ear to whatever might be said upon this subject. He had witnessed the beauty and happiness of a religious life, had become deeply impressed with the importance of the christian character, and had been trained to virtuous habits of conduct. While at Exeter he boarded with a

worthy and pious widow, who did not regard
her duty to her boarders as fully performed when
she had supplied their wants and satisfied their
appetites. She looked upon them as spiritual
and immortal beings, and was desirous of becoming an instrument in the hands of God in interesting them in the subject of religion. It was
her practice, during the time that Mr Whitman
boarded with her, to assemble her boarders
on Saturday evenings in her own room, where
one of them read from some book of practical
religion. Whitman was always a willing atten-
dant and ready assistant on these occasions,
and thus enjoyed good religious influence, tinged
though they were, and strongly too, with the
peculiarities of Calvinism. Then, too, during
the time he was at the Academy, there was in
Exeter much excitement upon the subject of
religion. This excitement reached his heart,
and took hold to some degree of his feelings.
And being connected, as it was, with Calvinistic
sentiments, he became, as a matter of course,
deeply interested in those views, and strongly
prejudiced against opinions of an opposite character. To illustrate this and show what were
his feelings at this time, extracts from two letters
to a sister are subjoined.

. Phillips Exeter Academy, Nov. 18, 1816.

"We have had most excellent preaching this term. Mr H. has supplied and has given such satisfaction that the people are about to invite him to settle with them. He is a fit example for any one to copy after, I think; not so *liberal* as Mr F., nor so *orthodox* as Mr R. We have many religious meetings of one kind and another, but principally orthodox. I do not attend them all, and when I do I call to mind the words of St Paul, "prove all things and hold fast that which is good." At this period he seems to have become somewhat interested, but not so much excited as to have forgotten the character, maxims and influence of his father, marked, as these were, by essential liberality, careful avoidance of party extremes, and entire devotion to scriptural guidance."

The next letter from which quotations will be made, indicates a greater degree of excitement. It is dated Phillips Exeter Academy, June 1st, 1817. It was an account of his return from Bridgewater to Exeter at the close of a vacation, at which time he spent one Sunday in Boston. Of this Sunday he says, "I attended meeting in the forenoon at Brattle street church, were I heard Dr R. In the afternoon I attended with one of my school-mates at the

Old South.   As Mr H. was on a journey for his
health, he had a preacher from the country,
whose name I did not learn.   He was not a very
eloquent man, but a far better preacher than
Dr R."

In this extract there is nothing of a very
decided character.   It shows, however, his pre-
dilections at the time.   In the same letter he
speaks as follows of the situation of things in a
religious point of view at Exeter upon his return.
" Mr H. is still preaching here where he is made
the means of doing much good.   A number of
young persons, besides those who had become
serious before I left, have since been awakened.
There has been a Mr O., an Episcopal minister,
preaching here, who is called a distinguished
pulpit orator, and a *truly pious* man ; likewise
a Mr A. is now preaching amongst us, a Baptist,
so that meetings are very frequent.   I have,
however, determined to attend only three evenings in a week, the evenings of Sunday, Tues-
day aud Friday, at the *regular lectures.*   I could
tell you of meetings, conversions and other
extraordinary things, which to you appear, I
suppose, as nothing or as something you do not
believe.   But I have seen, with my own eyes,
the effects of the operations of the Spirit.   I
have seen and known the different effects of

moral and of *Gospel* preaching. On this day nine students of Andover Academy are to be received into the church. And much more I could say on this subject, which you would call it foolish for me to write." In order that a proper degree of weight may be given to the extracts which have been made, it is necessary to state that the letter was addressed to a sister much older than himself, who had been to him as a mother, who had been for many years a professor of religion, and attached as he supposed to sentiments and modes of operation different from those in which he was now interested. There is no doubt then, but that he was restrained from expressing himself as he would have done under other circumstances. Yet there are sufficient indications of a highly excited state of the feelings, and a strong attachment to particular opinions. In the same letter there is still further and more decisive evidence of the sectarian prejudices of which he was at this time becoming the subject. For he writes as follows: " I have been invited to visit a number of places since I returned. At some of these places brother N., when here, was intimate. But I am afraid to go on his account, as it is reported here that he preached a sermon in W., if I mistake not, where Mr C. is settled, in

defence of the Unitarian doctrine, which he
carried very· far.   Much talk has been made
about it; I was told by a lady who heard it, and
she likewise said that *she* could made nothing
of it."

Thus it seems that, while Mr Whitman was
a student at Exeter, he became much excited
upon the subject of religion, and strongly prejudiced in favor of orthodox or Calvinistic opinions.   In conversation with an intimate friend
upon this subject, he attributed his not having
been entirely carried away at this time, to the
well timed advice and judicious treatment which
he received at the hands of his teacher, who,
without arousing his already excited feelings by
opposition, impressed upon his mind the importance of practical godliness, and referred him
to the scriptures as the standard of faith and
practice.

But, notwithstanding he was thus saved from
the extravagance of religious excitement, his
sectarian prejudices, at this time so strong, were
not easily nor soon removed.   For, not long
before his death, he stated to a brother, the Rev.
N. Whitman, in a very solemn and impressive
manner, that, when he entered Harvard College,
it was with a determination not to listen to nor
be influenced by the Unitarian preaching under

which he might there sit, and, that while present
in the chapel on the Sabbath, he used to court
sleep or fix his thoughts upon something foreign
from the place and the occasion, that 'so he
might escape the contamination of heresy.

In August, 1818, Mr Whitman left the Academy at Exeter for the University at Cambridge.
He was entered as a Freshman. He remained
connected with the University but little more
than one year. Of his character as developed
during this time something may be learned from
the following extracts from letters received from
classmates.

Says one, "I never knew him till we met at
a college exercise. We soon became intimate.
I was in the same section of the class with
him and heard his recitations. They manifested
great mental vigor and application. In a few
days he was ranked among the best scholars of
the class, and he maintained this standing as
long as he remained in it. But in his social
relations he was more distinguished than in the
recitation room. He was more matured than
most of the students, and his character was
already distinctly and strongly marked. At
that early stage of his education he gave decided
indications of the talents which he afterwards
so faithfully and so usefully employed. On

every proper occasion, he manifested the same
energy, courage and independence, which distinguished his professional life.   His classmates
respected his mind and loved his person.   He
soon acquired great popularity and influence
with them.   And it could not be otherwise, —
for, in addition to strong practical sense and
great force of character, he had that unfailing
good humor, which always conciliates the affections of generous youth.   With all mankind he
had ready sympathies, which easily grew into
warm friendship for those with whom he was
associated in the more intimate communion of
life.   Simplicity was perhaps the most remarkable feature of his outward character.   Without
being at all deficient in politeness, he was not
studious of refinement.   His manners were
perfectly unsophisticated.   I remember no symp-
tom of affectation of any kind.   He was always
fresh and natural, always himself.   There is no
doubt but that this quality greatly heightened
the influence of his short but active and earnest
life.   It brought his thoughts and feelings, just
as they were, into contact with other minds and
hearts.   The effect of his movements was never
impaired by any indirectness.   There was no
appearance of acting a part.   All that he said
or did was a free, open, honest manifestation of
his inmost soul.

"His moral and religious character was exemplary. Of his piety he was not ostentatious. He said little of his religious opinions, but I believe it was well understood that they were Calvinistic. I often heard him speak of the prevailing sentiments at the University in terms of strong and decided disapprobation, and I supposed that he entertained the common prejudices of the orthodox against Unitarians and Unitarianism."

Another classmate, in speaking of him says, "He was my classmate, and in the arrangement of the class we were placed together. This arbitrary and accidental connexion was accompanied by a union of our hearts in the bonds of sincere and lasting friendship. There are no traits in his character which were more impressed upon me than his benevolence and fidelity. He not only loved others, but he labored for their good. When he was at the Academy preparing for college, he was much older than the rest of the scholars, and he availed himself of the influence of his maturer years and superior experience, to befriend them in the most effectual way by giving them such advice as they needed, which advice was listened to with attention and docility, because he had first secured their confidence and affection. He was regarded by

5

them as an older brother, and when he left the Academy and entered the University, he did not forget them nor cease to labor for their improvement, but kept up a constant correspondence with them. I remember to have seen many long and affectionate and excellent letters, written by him to the lads whom he left at the Academy, who will ever remember with gratitude the benefit they thus derived from his faithful and disinterested and most valuable friendship. I have no hesitation in saying that he was *universally* beloved, esteemed, and confided in by his associates at the Academy and at College, as well as in all other parts and scenes of his life."

From these extracts we have learned the rank in scholarship which Mr Whitman acquired, the character which he maintained, and the esteem in which be was held during the short period of his connexion with the University. We now pass to the circumstances of his leaving that institution. The account of these will be given in the language of a classmate. He says, " Early in the Sophomore year, our class had one of those epidemic excitements, which often begin in enthusiasm and end in sorrow. The rebellion of 1818, to call it by its common name, originated in a kind of mock fight between the

Sophomore and Freshmen classes in Commons hall. Some of the officers attempted to restore order and their authority was disregarded. In consequence of this, two students were suspended for several months. They happened to be fine young men, and very popular with the class. It is not supposed that the Government acted hastily or improperly, but the class were angry, and therefore unreasonable. I had been out of town. I returned just as the suspended students were sent away. I found the class in a state of extreme excitement, in which your brother pro-bably shared, for one of the punished was his most intimate friend and room-mate. The class now determined, if possible, to bring the Gov-ernment to terms. They resolved, with I think but one exception, to attend no recitation until the two suspended students should be recalled. There was a general gathering under an elm called the rebellion tree, and some inflammatory speeches and shouting and uproar, and so it ended on their part. But it did not so end on the part of the Government. It was necessary to restore discipline. But, where the offence is so general, it is difficult to make a selection. After a long deliberation, a few were rusticated, a few suspended, and all the rest of the dis-affected class dismissed from College. The

last were soon readmitted on their promise to
submit to the laws. Your brother was among
the few who were rusticated. How far he
entered into the excited feeling of the class I
have no means of ascertaining. It is not to be
supposed that the Government imputed any
special blame to those who fell under their spe-
cific censures. Punishment must be inflicted
on some, and under circumstances which made
a nice discrimination impossible. I have had
opportunity to know that some individuals were
punished, because they were supposed to have
influence, which ought to have been exerted in
allaying the excitement among their classmates.

After pursuing his studies for a year in private,
your brother was admitted into college again.
But college was not what it had been to him.
He was separated from the class he loved, all
his pleasing associations were disturbed. He
took an honorable dismission, and departed to
finish his education elsewhere. How well he
completed it, and how nobly he used it, I need
not say. 'The community that mourns his loss
will not forget his works."

Such were the circumstances under which
Mr Whitman left College. The year, during
which he was under college censure, was spent
in the faithful pursuit of his studies, with the

exception of three months in the winter; these he spent in Scituate, Mass., as a teacher in a common town school. A small portion of the year was spent in Canton, Mass., that he might enjoy, in his mathematical studies, the instruction of Mr Warren Colburn, who was at that time teaching in that place. The remainder of the time was spent in the family of the clergyman in East Bridgewater. Of the manner in which that time was employed and of his general conduct and character while there, the clergyman thus writes : — " Your brother passed in my family, as you know, most of the time during which he was under the censure of the college government. His conduct was perfectly exemplary while with me. His application to the studies of his class, and in pursuit of knowledge in general, was such as needed a check rather than any incitement from me. He secured the warmest regard and attachment of all my family. He never complained of the censure he had incurred, though, under the impulse of the moment, he felt that the occasion justified the part he took with his excited associates. He cherished the hope, that, from his previous deportment, which had been very satisfactory to the government, and the manner in which he had improved his year of banishment from col-

lege, he should be restored to his class, and that
the part of his punishment, which required him
to take his place in a class below, would be
rescinded. He was willing to make every proper
acknowledgement of his error, but he could not
bring himself to appear among his associates,
as a degraded member of the community in
which he had so long held a distinguished rank
in scholarship and good character. I warmly
interested myself to obtain the remission of this
part of his punishment from the college government, but, without success. He accordingly
dissolved his connexion with college, immediately after having been examined and admitted
to the class below."

It has been deemed necessary to state thus
particularly the circumstances of Mr Whitman's
leaving the University, in order to develop more
fully the peculiarities of his character, and to
point out more accurately the successive influences under which it was formed. It will be
perceived that his conduct on this occasion was
in perfect keeping with all the previous manifestations of his character. He was from a
child ardent in his temperament, a lover of
justice, bold in resisting oppression, strong in
his attachments to his friends, and resolute in
the defence of their rights. Those who know

the delusions under which college students labor
in a time of rebellion, will perceive that, to his
mind, at that time, it appeared that his intimate
friend and room-mate was unjustly punished.
This was precisely the view to call forth all the
ardor of his temperament, all the strength of
his attachment to his friend, all his love of justice
and hatred of oppression, and arouse him to
acts of open opposition. As might have been
anticipated, he partook in no small degree of
the excitement which prevailed among his classmates. He labored, it is true, under a strange
delusion, a delusion which he afterwards felt
and acknowledged. But it was an error of the
judgment, not a perversion of heart. The
purity of his feelings, and the uprightness of his
purposes remained the same.

But the abrupt termination of his collegiate
course was a circumstance calculated to exert
a powerful influence upon his whole subsequent
conduct, his whole future character. He had
entered college with high hopes and honorable
desires of distinction. He was pursuing his
course with gratifying success. Fair prospects
were beginning to open before him. His bright
hopes and pleasing anticipations were at once
blasted. He was thrown back upon himself.
He had none among the rich, powerful, or

learned, to whom he could look as his patrons.
He had no means of support even, other than
his own efforts, on which to rely. He had cut
himself off from the advantages of a regular
collegiate education, and had excited in the
minds of many in the community, suspicions in
regard to his character. Under circumstances
like these, most would have yielded in despair,
or have been urged onwards in their efforts by
feelings of bitterness and animosity towards the
University they had left. But not so with the
subject of this memoir. The thought of yielding
in despair, never, it is presumed, once occurred
to him. He had learned in early life to rely
upon himself. His self-reliance was now called
into new and more vigorous exercise, and was
thus strengthened and confirmed. He remained
apparently calm and cheerful. He was, indeed,
the subject of deep and powerful emotions, of
inward grief and anxiety and sorrow. But he
confined these feelings to his own breast, he
gave no expression to them, and endeavored to
overcome them by persevering diligence in his
studies. He engaged in labors as a teacher for
his support, and studied as faithfully as his circumstances and time would permit. In consequence of leaving college as he did, he lost all
the influence and patronage of the friends of

the college, which he might otherwise have enjoyed. Whatever he was, he was only what, under apparently adverse circumstances, he made himself. Whatever of rank he obtained, it was not the gift of his friends, it was the result and the reward of his own exertions. But while struggling against obstacles, which were consequent upon his leaving college, he never permitted himself to harbor one unkind wish, a single bitter feeling, towards the institution he had left. He was a true and fast friend to the college, vindicating its character from the aspersions of enemies, and urging upon his young friends the importance of availing themselves of its advantages. He was, in this way, instrumental in influencing several to enter there, who would have entered elsewhere, or have gone to their professions without a regular collegiate education.

There is another particular in regard to which the circumstance of his leaving college exerted a powerful influence. His early life, it has been said, was spent among the people. He was one of them, — he had learned their modes of thinking and speaking, and knew how to approach and address them. But it is often the case, that those, whose early life is passed in these circumstances, forget, when they become interested in literary pursuits, the impressions of their early years and the modes of thinking and speaking once familiar to them. They form the habit, while acquiring their education, of using abstract terms and generalizing their statements, and of employing, not the words and modes of expression which are of common and every day use among the people, but those which are in accordance with the usage of standard writers. There is reason to believe that such would have been the case with Mr Whitman had he remained through the college course. For his style, even in the short time he was a member of college, was gradually forming itself into a general and abstract, but ornamental and beautiful style. But he was taken at once from exclusive devotion to pursuits entirely literary, and thrown back to mingle again among the mass of his fellow men. In these circumstances he learned to estimate style, not by its resemblance to standard authors, but by its adaptation to its appropriate purpose, the communication of ideas. This produced an entire change in his ideas as to the kind of style best adapted to do good among the great mass of the community, and recalled and deepened all his early impressions in regard to the modes of reasoning, thinking and speaking among them. Under the influence of the circumstances into which he was now thrown, and aided by the faithful instructions of a subsequent teacher, he did succeed in entirely changing his style of writing, from one most natural to himself, to one which seemed most useful to the community. An extract from a letter written by one of his classmates in relation to this point, the change which took place in his style may with propriety be introduced here. The writer, speaking of some letters from Mr Whitman to himself, written during the time he was under college censure, says, " You will discern in them those evidences of ardor of affection, purity of mind, love of truth, sincerity of heart, active industry, resoluteness of purpose, and pervading piety of spirit, which were equally and uniformly manifested throughout the virtuous, useful and important life of your lamented brother. In reading them, I have been struck with one circumstance they disclose. Your brother, as a theological writer and preacher, excelled particularly his cotemporaries in the clearness, simplicity, directness and plainness of his style. He aimed to write and speak so as to be understood, at once and equally, by all. He had no idea of ornamenting his style, of making a rhetorical display, of getting the name of ' a fine writer.' · Yet, if you examine these letters, you will find that, while acquiring his education and when he wrote without practice or cultivation, his style was remarkable for its richness and for the evidence which it gives of a most brilliant and affluent imagination. He seems to have foreseen the path, in which, as a writer, he was destined to pursue so useful a career in the defence and diffusion of religious truth, and to have entirely altered and reconstructed his style of composition. He might have been eminent amongst our most eloquent and elegant writers. He might have secured admiration as a genius. But he preferred to be useful rather than celebrated among his fellow men, and while he accomplished his great purpose in becoming eminently useful, he was no doubt surprised as much as he was gratified at the celebrity he obtained. While he never resorted to his imagination to embellish his style, the faculty was of singular use to him, in suggesting readily and - abundantly those apt but familiar illustrations, by which he was accustomed to render still clearer and more intelligible the truths and arguments which he was inculcating in his plain and forcible language."

About the time of Mr Whitman's leaving the University, and during the period he was under college censure, he became somewhat interested in the writings of Emanuel Swedenborg. He procured and read several of his works, and was becoming quite intimate with some of his followers. He never, it is true, became what is technically called " a receiver of the doctrines." The reasons of this, assigned by him in casual conversation in after life, were these : He could not regard Swedenborg as a messenger and interpreter inspired of God, and therefore could not receive his instructions as authoritative. He was obliged to regard them but as the speculations of a man. Consequently, in reading his writings he felt himslf in duty bound to examine, and sift, and judge of them for himself. In doing this, while he found much that was true and beautiful and valuable, he also found much which he regarded as trash. And then, too, he found, as he became better acquainted with other religious systems, that what was true and beautiful and valuable in the writings of Swedenborg, was not peculiar to nor necessarily connected with that system. His religious feelings and character became at this time, and partly it may be in consequence of these influences, materially changed. His zeal for opinions and his sectarian peculiarities gave place to a deep interest in the spirituality and benevolence

6

of the Gospel. It was because he discovered something of these in the writings of Swedenborg that he was interested in them. He ever looked back, it is believed, with gratitude to the change experienced at this time; he often spoke of the beautiful and the true in the writings of Swedenborg, and in the views of his followers. Yet he was willing, and at one time determined, in his devotion to the service of one greater than Swedenborg, to point out the errors and follies which encumber his views, in a series of letters to his followers. The consequence of the change, which he at this time experienoed, was to fill him with zeal for the spiritual and the benevolent, to lead him to acknowledge these as the legitimate fruits of gospel influences in whatever denomination they might appear, and to value and contend for truth only as the divinely appointed means of cherishing the spiritual and the benevolent in individual hearts.

During the period of his absence from college, he began to look more anxiously upon the course which was before him in the profession of his choice. He saw the christian community divided into various sects, and he felt that every student for the ministry was subjected to influences among contending denominations, calculated to draw him aside from entire and unreserved devotion to truth. The writer of this memoir found afterwards among some loose papers in the room which he had occupied at his father's, a slip, written, as it would seem, in full view and with particular reference to this danger. It contained a resolution, accompanied by a prayer, that in the study of his profession, he would carefully guard against becoming the visible follower of any man or body of men, but would make the sacred scriptures, in the careful and prayerful study of them, his only guide.

This chapter, touching as it does upon the circumstances of Mr Whitman's leaving the University, ought not to be closed without giving his subsequent feelings upon the subject of college rebellions. And this can best be done by simply stating a fact. The subject and the writer of this memoir, once planned a book to be prepared by them in connexion, to be entitled "Letters to College Students." In making the arrangements as to the particular subjects upon which each one should write, Bernard said that he would take the letter on *Rebellions*, because he thought that from his own experience, he could make the folly and sinfulness of them stand out so fully to view as to produce a strong impression upon the mind, and he wished to do something to deter others from the errors and follies into which he had himself fallen. Should the name of Bernard Whitman, then, ever be quoted by a rebellious student as one, who, notwithstanding his loss of college advantages and honors and patronage, still succeeded in life, let there always be added to the quotation, the thought that this same Bernard Whitman, amid all his success in after life, was most fully sensible of the utter folly of college rebellions, and most sincerely regretted the part he had taken in them.

CHAPTER III.

Opens a private school in Billerica, Mass. — His interest while there in the general improvement of all with whom he associated — Goes to Welfleet, Mass. to pursue his professional studies under the direction of the clergyman — Leaves Welfleet and takes charge of the Academy in Sandwich, Mass. for a few months — His character as a teacher — Leaves Sandwich and removes to Beverly to pursue and complete his professional studies under the direction of Rev. Abiel Abbott, D. D. — Testimony in regard to his character and active interest in the best good of all around — Takes charge of the Academy in Billerica for a few months — Is approbated to preach — Preaches in several different places, and is finally settled in Waltham, Mass.

It was in the autumn of the year 1819, that Mr Whitman received an honorable dismission from the University, and gave up the long cherished hope of a collegiate education. He was now compelled to seek for some employment, which would furnish the means of support and at the same time afford him an opportunity to pursue his studies and prepare for the profession of his choice. The business of teaching seemed best to comport with his desires. He went to

6*

Billerica, Mass., where an older brother, the
Rev. N. Whitman, was then settled in the ministry, and opened a private school. As a teacher
he was successful and popular. He was not
one, who regarded the teacher's task as consisting simply in watching his pupils to see that
they were faithful in their prescribed lessons
and correct in their conduct during the hours
of school. He looked upon all committed to
his charge as beings who might enjoy pure and
refined happiness in the exercise of the mind
and heart if these should be rightly cultivated
and improved. Consequently, it was the great
object of all his efforts to awaken each individual of his pupils to a proper sense of the importance of intellectual improvement, and to aid
and guide them in their endeavors to form for
themselves correct tastes and habits. He had
none of the sternness and severity once supposed
to be necessary for the pedagogue, but manifested in its stead all the interest and all the
kindness of a brother.

He did not confine his attention, while in
Billerica, to his school. He found there a circle
of young ladies. Some of them were at first
among the oldest of his pupils. They were
just at the age when most in danger from frivo-
lous tastes and habits. He saw at once, and

clearly, the dangers to which they were exposed, and put forth all his exertions in endeavors to awaken within them an interest in something higher and purer and nobler than mere fashion and frivolity. He was instrumental in forming these young ladies into a society or " Social Circle," for their mutual intellectual, moral and religious improvement. The members of this circle spent their time, while together, in reading, either from some work previously selected, or from themes and essays prepared by the members themselves, and in conversation upon what they read. It was Mr Whitman's endeavor to interest them in books of an improving kind, and to accustom them, by the practice of writing, to reflect upon what they might read, to digest it and make it their own, by incorporating it with the results of their own thoughts. And his object was to furnish them, in this way, with the means of happiness within themselves, that so they might be independent of outward changes. He was not satisfied with merely forming them into an association. He was careful to guide, as far as he might, their reading, that so he might guard them from that worse than waste of time, the excessive and indiscriminate reading of novels. His views, in regard to the kind of reading he would recommend, may perhaps be indicated by the circumstance, that he presented to this " Social Circle" the works of Miss H. More. This association was formed for the mutual, intellectual, moral, and *religious* improvement of its members. Nor was religious improvement left, as is too often the case, to take care of itself, or expected to follow as a natural consequence from an attention to intellectual and moral culture. It was their custom to spend a portion of the time they were together in direct attention to religious subjects, in reading the sacred scriptures, religious books, or original essays upon religious subjects, and in conversation upon what they read. With the members of this society he spent much time, for their good he labored much, furnishing something from his own pen at almost every meeting. Every one of them regarded him, it is believed, as a brother, and will attribute much of their personal improvement to his exertions. Nor did he forget them when he left the place. For years afterwards did he manifest his interest in them by frequent and long letters. In confirmation of what is here stated in regard to his interest in and labors for this circle of young ladies, an extract from a letter received from one of its members is here added. "As it respects our

little band of sisters, our *Social Circle*, his efforts
for their advancement in social, moral, intellectual and religious improvement were untiring,
yea, almost without a parallel. You, doubtless,
recollect the method he adopted to effect their
improvement, assisting them in composition and
directing them in a judicious course of reading.
It has appeared to me, that, from the exercise
of his own masterly and powerful mind, there
emanated a sort of stimulus, which was more
or less infused into the minds of all who enjoyed his intimate acquaintance. As it re-
spcots myself individually, his memory is em-
balmed with the deepest feelings of gratitude
for the interest he ever manifested in my improvement during the period I had the happiness
of being his pupil. Upon this subject, could I
embody my feelings in words, no doubt those
who knew him less intimately would charge me
with enthusiasm."

It cannot be supposed, that with the arduous
labors consequent upon a large school, together
with the interest which he took in the general
improvement of society around him, Mr Whitman found much time for close study. Yet his
reading at this period, which was pursued under
the advice of his brother, was of a kind calculated to establish his mind, settle the foundations

of his faith, and prepare him for the more successful pursuit of studies directly preparatory to his profession. His attention was directed to solid works on the foundations, evidences, and outlines of Christianity.

In the autumn of 1821, Mr Whitman left Billerica to enter upon the more direct and devoted pursuit of his professional studies. He spent a few months at his father's house in East Bridgewater, and then removed to Welfleet, Mass., and placed himself under the instruction of Rev. Timothy Davis, as a student in Theology. As Mr Davis was a known and decided Calvinist, Mr Whitman's placing himself under his instruction would seem to be an indication of his sentiments at this time. But an inference drawn from this indication would be incorrect. He was at this time an inquirer, a seeker after truth. The foundation of his religious character, as has been already intimated, was laid in early life. His parents had endeavored to communicate religious knowledge, implant religious principles, and form virtuous habits. But in doing this, they communicated their own sentiments in precisely the shape in which they existed in their own minds, as gospel truths, and not as sectarian peculiarities. It was their wish, also, to see their children religious in

principle and conduct, rather than to hear them
speaking often upon the subject of religious
feelings. The elements of the religious char-
-acter in the subject of this memoir, when he
left the paternal roof, so far as they had at that
early period become developed, were in accordance with these views and wishes. At Exeter
he was introduced to an acquaintance with what
was to him an entirely new manifestation of religion. He heard much talk upon the subject of
peculiar religious feelings, and special spiritual
operations and assistances, and witnessed much
zeal for sectarian peculiarities of opinion. The
effect upon his mind was perfectly natural. He
felt as if he had never before witnessed a true
manifestation of religious influences, and he
became excited. His excitement resulted in
increased controversial and sectarian zeal, accompanied indeed by a deepened and more
constantly pervading interest in personal religion. When he became acquainted with Sweden-
borgianism, he was introduced to a still different
manifestation of religion, a manifestation of the
spirit of holy love. Religion now appeared to
him to be something far different from, and far
higher than mere zeal for religions opinions, to
consist in personal holiness both in thought and
deed, and in active benevolence in all the rela-

tions of life. On becoming convinced that
personal holiness and active benevolence were
common to the truly religious of all denominations, he laid aside his zeal for a sect, and became zealous for the gospel according to his
knowledge of its character, irrespective of all
parties. This was his state of mind when he
went to Welfleet. The principal reason of his
selecting this place was, that here he could
board in the family of an older brother, a deacon in Mr Davis's church, and in this way be
favored in a pecuniary point of view. But he
went with a fixed determination to study the
Bible for himself, and be independent of all
sects in the formation of his religious opinions.
Mr Davis advised him to take Scott's Family
Bible as his guide, inasmuch as Scott had gathered and condensed most that was valuable in
other commentators. This advice was not in
accordance with the natural boldness of Mr
Whitman's mind in the search of truth, nor
with the determination, under which he was
acting, to read the Bible for himself. While at
Welfleet, Mr Whitman occasionally took part
in meetings for conference and exhortation.
And thus he enjoyed an opportunity of learning
the importance of the utmost plainness and
directness of address, and of the most clear and

perceptible connexion between premises and conclusions, when addressing the less informed portion of the community upon the subject of religion, while at the same time he exercised and improved himself in extemporaneous speaking. In this, as in other respects, he was much benefitted by his stay in Welfleet. It was while here that he made an open profession of his faith in Christ. As he had no fixed residence, and his character had become known in Billerica, he connected himself with the church in that place. He was propounded and admitted on the ground of a written statement of his belief, wishes and purposes. But as he still considered himself a learner in the school of Christ, bound to continue his search for further acquaintance with truth as well as for a better knowledge of duty, there was nothing in it very important in regard to his religious opinions.

In the spring of 1822 Mr Whitman left Welfleet and took charge, for three months, of the academy in Sandwich, Mass. All that is known of him, to the writer, while there is contained in the following extract from a letter written by one who was at that time one of his pupils. "If I remember rightly," he says, "he was preceptor of the academy at Sandwich only about three months, in the summer of 1822. He delivered

7

an oration on the fourth of July that year, at Sandwich, which was listened to with great pleasure by a crowded assembly. The impressions he made upon me at that time, as an instructor, are still vivid in my recollection. He was the first teacher whom I looked upon as a personal friend. He was remarkable for feeling and manifesting a strong interest in each of his pupils. And I believe that they all felt a corresponding interest in him. He had the happy faculty of exciting the backward and dull and of encouraging the timid and doubting. In his discipline he was not severe but faithful and exact. And we all had a suitable mixture of a fear of giving offence with a strong regard and sincere love for the man."

Upon leaving Sandwich, Mr Whitman removed to Beverly, Mass., where he placed himself under the instruction of Rev. Abiel Abbott, D. D. Here he remained until he had completed his Theological studies. When he went to Beverly, his habits of study and his style of writing needed much correction. From his various changes during the two or three last years, both in pursuits and in places of residence, he had become desultory in his habits of study. And, although he had formed correct ideas of the object to be aimed at in writing, and of the kind of style best adapted to the community, yet, in the absence of any one to guide, counsel and direct him, and with but little opportunity for careful revision of what he wrote, his style had actually become very loose, diffuse, and in many instances, from these circumstances, somewhat involved. Dr Abbott was very faithful in his exertions for Mr Whitman's improvement in everything that might serve to prepare him for usefulness in his profession. Mr Whitman boarded, while in Beverly, with a widow lady, that he might pay for his board by instructing her only son. But he was a very frequent visitor in Dr Abbott's family, and was received there with all the cordiality of a son and a brother. The Dr. was free and familiar with him in all his conversations upon ministerial faithfulness and prudence, and upon the peculiarities of a minister's trials, responsibilities and duties, both as a teacher and a pastor. In regard to his sermons, Dr Abbott compelled him to a very free use of the "*pruning* knife." It was his custom to examine them with all the care, with which a school-boy's composition or a collegian's theme are, usually examined, and then to require them to be written out again in a corrected form. Indeed, very much is due to Dr Abbott. Had it not been for his more

than usually faithful labors, Mr Whitman would
never have been so useful nor so distinguished
as he afterwards became. , Dr Abbott has gone
to the reward of his labors, and therefore we
cannot learn from his own lips or pen what were
his impressions in regard to Mr Whitman at
that time. To supply this deficiency, extracts
from a letter written by one who was acquainted
with them both, are subjoined. " I recollect,"
he says, " hearing the late Dr Abbott, with
whom he was then pursuing his Theological
studies, speak of him in terms of high commendation and augur very favorably of his future
usefulness in the christian ministry. The only
fear I ever heard him express in regard to it
was, lest the ardor of his disposition, combined
with his unguarded frankness of temper and
speech, might expose him to misconstruction on
the part of others and to consequent difficulty.
I further recollect hearing Dr A. remark, that
Mr Whitman's style of writing underwent a
great change while he was at Beverly, that in
his compositions during the earlier part of his
residence there, instead of the simplicity, clearness, directness and strength which afterwards
characterized his productions, the sentences
were often long, involved, and occasionally
somewhat obscure ; and that to such a degree

as to render sermons so written in some measure unintelligible to a considerable portion of almost every religious congregation." The fears of Dr A. alluded to in the above extract, were perfectly natural, and probably suggested the topics of the charge which he gave Mr Whitman at his ordination. The title of that charge was " 'The union of *prudence*, *fidelity* and *zeal*, the duty of Ministers."

In Beverly Mr Whitman enjoyed an opportunity of exercising, and thereby strengthening and cherishing his already strongly marked characteristic of active benevolence. He found there a circle of young ladies just at the age when they are peculiarly interesting and peculiarly exposed to danger; and when, consequently, it was of the utmost importance that they should enjoy the counsel and advice of some judicious friend, in whom they had confidence. He soon became to the young ladies in Beverly the same kind friend, counsellor, guide and brother, which he had been to those in Billerica. But in regard to this, it is more proper that one, who was of the number of these young ladies, should speak. " I was quite young when your brother came to Beverly, exactly at that period of life, when, though we are not qualified to appreciate character justly, we are unconsciously attentive to the development of it. From observations then made, we, in riper years, form comparisons and draw conclusions, and thus in the end come properly to understand the characters of those with whom we associated, long, perhaps, after all intercourse with them has ceased. And thus it was with me in regard to your brother. 1 saw him frequently, being very intimate in a family where much of his time was naturally spent. He very 'soon expressed an interest in my intellectual and moral improvement. And I have since been aware, that he had much to do with the cultivation of my mind and heart at that period, principally by directing my miscellaneous reading, when I was a greedy devourer of books. And grateful indeed do I now feel for the kindness which prompted him to select reading for me from his own well chosen books, directing my attention to their real merits, and thus, perhaps, preserving me at that important age, from the 'trash of circulating libraries.' I then looked up to him with confidence and affectionate regard as I should to an elder brother, and his truly benevolent heart was highly gratified, when he found that he had awakened these feelings in his young friends at Beverly. I now think of him as one of the most generous and

warm hearted men I have ever known. He
was always inclined to think well rather than
ill of others, highly appreciating their good
qualities, and strongly condemning, but without
bitterness, their evil ones, when forced upon his
notice. I never knew one who felt a deeper
reverence for the virtue of sincerity. The
very shadow of duplicity was an abomination in
his eyes. His love of independence was then
as afterwards, a prominent trait in his character.
Indeed, so unwilling was he to be trammelled
by the erroneous or illiberal views of others,
that he sometimes, perhaps, approached the
verge of imprudence. He was remarkable for
the equanimity of his temper, unvarying cheerfulness marking his deportment at all times.
At the period in which these impressions of his
character were made upon my mind, the minor
trials and perplexities of life had no power to
disturb his serenity beyond the passing moment;
and certainly, in after experience, its weightier
afflictions, instead of depressing his spirit, but
elevated it to perfect resignation and trust in
God."

" His endeavor to promote social, cheerful and
rational intercourse in the circle in which he
moved at Beverly, will long be remembered.
He was, I believe, the first to propose the plan

of a Reading Party, which became very popular
and was continued for three or four years with
almost unabated interest, and which proved, as
I think, a source of no little intellectual improvement, as well as of social enjoyment, to its
various members. When he left Beverly, he
was universally regretted in this circle, and he
yet lives in its affectionate remembrance. Our
friendship did not cease on his removal from
Beverly. I passed three weeks in his family in
Waltham in the autumn of 1828, and there had
fresh opportunities of observing his character,
which served only to deepen my respect for him.
I then saw him applying to practice, on an extended scale, the same principles of benevolence
and virtue, which he had recommended in the
earlier days of our acquaintance ; and this
tended to perpetuate the influence which he had
exercised over my mind." In confirmation of
these statements, an extract may be added from
a letter written by a gentleman, who became a
resident in Beverly a short time before Mr Whitman's departure, and who remained to witness
the effects of his influence there, he says : " He
(Mr Whitman) seems to me to have exerted a
very salutary influence upon the minds of many
young persons in Beverly, by imparting to them
something of his own thirst for moral and intel-

lectual excellence. His lively sympathies, his
ardent feelings, his active and benevolent disposition, combined with strong good sense and
a peculiar practical turn of mind, prompted and
enabled him to do much to diffuse, especially
among the young ladies with whom he associated,
a desire for mental improvement and a taste for
intellectual pursuits, the effects of which were
visible long after his departure from the town.
It is not my purpose to attempt a sketch of his
character, but I cannot forbear to observe, that
together with a sincerity above all disguise,
unvarying cheerfulness, and unpretending simplicity of manners, there was united in his social
character a remarkable degree of what might
be termed good nature, which placed all at ease
in his society, and invited and justified confidence in his disposition to oblige at the sacrifice
of almost any time, labor, or convenience."

It has been said that while at Beverly Mr
Whitman boarded with a widow, that so he
might instruct her son. Something more may
be learned, in regard to his character, from a
letter written by that son. "I remember perfectly well the first evening I ever saw him.
Dr Abbott had proposed to my mother to take
him to board, that so I might pursue my studies
under his direction. I was then about eleven

years old, had seen but few strangers, and stood in great awe of them, and particularly of clerical people. Dr Abbott introduced him about tea time. He took tea with us, and before it was half over I felt the same sort of familiar respect for him that I felt for my uncle. From that moment till the day of his death, I never had any other feelings towards him than towards an elder brother, possessing every claim upon my confidence and affection. His whole domestic life, while with my mother, was such as to endear him, to an unprecedented degree, to her and all her friends. He was peculiarly ready to accommodate, anxious to avoid giving trouble, always satisfied and pleased with everything, and apparently as delicately attentive to my mother's health and comfort, as if she had been his own mother. Frequently did he volunteer to do for her services (such as shovelling paths in winter, &c.) which my strength would not permit me to perform, and which would otherwise have caused her much trouble as well as some expense. He was very much straitened in his pecuniary affairs while at Beverly. His wardrobe was in such a state as to keep some portion or other of it almost constantly under the operation of the needle. Month after month he spent no money except that he would occa-

sionally borrow fourpence of my mother to pay
his toll to Salem. Yet these things never seemed in the least to depress his spirits. He seemed
perfectly easy and happy. He used to speak of
his old coat and cloak as grounds of pride.
Having earned them, he said that he should
wear them as long as he could, for he took more
pleasure in wearing an old coat that was paid
for, than a new one unpaid for. In apparel and
in everything that concerned personal display,
his utter indifference rather than his poverty
kept him rigidly economical in all his expenses.
In all expenses of a social or intellectual character, books, visiting, charitable objects of all
kinds, his contempt for money permitted him to
be extravagant, so that with maxims of prudence
often upon his lips, I have no doubt that the
expenditures for which he made himself liable
at that time, were much greater than they ought
to have been.

"Your brother was the most benevolent, obliging man I ever saw. That early became known
to his acquaintance at Beverly, and numerous
daily drafts were made upon his time and labor
for the sole benefit of others, and never were
the drafts protested. When he could oblige any
one else, he never seemed to think of his own in-
convenience or engagements. Scarcely is there

an individual among his acquaintance at Beverly,
who ever speaks of him without recurring to
repeated instances of personal attention and
kindness. He did much for the improvement
of society there. He did much towards cherishing a taste for reading and study, was forward
in the establishment of a reading circle, circulated books, and periodicals, and introduced
conversation on subjects of an elevating and
improving character. I can see most distinctly,
even now, the traces of his spirit. He was
always cautious in regard to his moral influence,
at great pains that it might be of a right and
good character. To the young men of the
town his society was always particularly pleasing,
as he never assumed a dictatorial tone, but always mingled amusement and instruction, and
at the same time gave them valuable information
and left a good moral impression. Of the esteem in which he was held by those who knew
him, the fact that, in addition to numerous small
tokens, the ladies of the place gave him a valuable present of clothing before his departure,
will furnish some proof. Of his kindness to
myself I can never think without the warmest
gratitude, and I know that I owe to him the
cure of some faults, which might have ripened
into vices. I wonder that he bore with me so

much or so long. But he never once gave me a harsh rebuke and always spared my mother the recital of my childish failings. He contrived however to shew me his sense of my conduct in such a way as to make me feel deeply his kindness in contrast with it, and always took care to place before me better examples and right maxims of conduct; and to the gradual and silent influence of his counsels and kindness I am much indebted.

Your brother was characterized while at Beverly by a supreme indifference to all artificial, conventional restraints, and prejudices. And by this indifference, by studying no other limits of conduct than those of positive right and wrong, while he had many friends, he had many slanderers, and probably enjoyed little esteem from the most rigidly circumspect of Dr Abbot's society,—while he was the subject of devout antipathy to the orthodox portion of the community. I think that his character was at that time exceedingly faulty in this one point, that he paid no regard whatever to his own interest or reputation. Every social virtue he cultivated and manifested; purity and integrity and piety, he made the laws of his own soul and conduct. But I do not believe that providence, prudence, care of reputation, reference

to future means and power of usefulness, in
any sense or degree, then formed a part of his
character. These traits, subsequent intercourse
with the world seems in some measure to have
formed, but even to the last, it seems to me,
that he was not only devoid of selfishness, but
that he was deficient in an enlightened and prudent self-love."

From these extracts Mr Whitman's character while at Beverly may be gathered. Some
time during the summer of 1834, the Preceptor
of Billerica Academy was obliged by ill-health
to leave his labors. Mr Whitman stepped in to
supply his place for the remainder of the term.
While here he received approbation as a
preacher, and commenced the public labors of
his profession. He preached in several neighboring pulpits and was regarded as a young
man of considerable promise. In the autumn
of the same year he took rooms at Cambridge,
but was not permitted to remain long there.
He preached for a time in Keene, N. H., and
then engaged to supply for six months the pulpit in Middlesex Village, so called, in the town
of Chelmsford, Mass. He here found a person
struggling with a country newspaper — not able
to make his paper interesting and to secure
subscribers without the labors of an editor, and

not able to offer such compensation as to secure those labors. Wishing to render this man some assistance, Mr Whitman at once, without the hope of compensation, with no prospect of advantage to himself, assumed the editorship of this paper and labored diligently in its management. He at once changed the character of the paper from that of a mere vehicle of gossip, to that of an instrument in the promotion of the social, moral and intellectual improvement of its readers. The motto which he adopted, as well as the peculiar circumstances of his connexion with the paper, is in perfect keeping with his all-grasping feelings of benevolence. It was, *" Devoted to everything good."* Having completed his engagement at Chelmsford, he preached at Duxbury, and excited so much interest, that many were extremely desirous that he should settle with them in the ministry. But while they were making preparations tending to this, he received an invitation to become the pastor of the second religious society in Waltham, Mass. This invitation he accepted and was ordained on the 15th of February, 1826.

CHAPTER IV.

His feelings and resolutions in regard to his future course — these are modified by the circumstances in which he was placed — The circumstances which led to his successive publications — Remarks on the character of his writings — His character as a preacher — His own views in regard to preaching — His exertions for the general improvement of his people — His marriage — The character and influence of his wife — The circumstances of her sickness and death — His second marriage — His efforts and character as a missionary — His influence in encouraging young men to enter the ministry — His ministerial intercourse with Restorationists — His fertility in plans for improvement — His character as a member of ministerial associations — His invitations to leave his people — His feelings in regard to them and his treatment of them — His views in regard to various public movements — His exertions in the cause of temperance — His sickness and death — Notices of his character.

We have traced the course of Mr Whitman from early childhood to his settlement in the ministry, have become acquainted with the difficulties with which he was called to contend, and with the influences under which his character had thus far been formed. We now enter upon the more public and important part of his life. Here it will be inconvenient to be guided by a strict regard to chronological order. We must treat of the various topics and characteristics in the order in which they may present themselves.

Every one, it is presumed, who enters the Christian ministry and takes charge of a religions society, cherishes peculiar feelings and forms peculiar plans in regard to his future course. Such was the case with Mr Whitman. His plans and feelings as expressed by himself in a conversation with the writer, were as follows. He intended to confine and devote himself to the advancement of what he regarded as the best interests of his own people. He had no thought of becoming an author or of laboring for the public. The ways in which he then intended to labor for the best interests of his people were, by plain, direct and practical preaching, by encouraging in every possible way their general, social, intellectual and moral improvement, and by faithful parochial visitation. In short, it was his intention to become as far as possible a faithful parish minister. But feelings and plans like these are merely theoretical. They are based upon abstract views of the

duties of the ministry. They seldom have
reference to the peculiar circumstances under
which these duties are to be performed. It
often happens, therefore, that the peculiar circumstances and character of the people over
whom one is placed, and even the tone of the
services at his ordination, give a turn and com-
plexion to his subsequent ministerial course entirely different from his previous plans and
feelings. Such was, in some degree, the case
with Mr Whitman. He was ordained under
peculiar circumstances. When the Cotton
Manufactories were established in Waltham,
they were instrumental in adding largely to the
population of the place. And as the people
connected with the manufacturing establishment
differed in habits and feelings from the farmers
by whom the town was previously principally
inhabited, they did not unite with the religious
society already established. A new society
was formed and a new house of worship erected.
This was before the lines of separation between
the Orthodox and Unitarian denominations had
been distinctly drawn. This new society embraced some of both classes. The Rev. Sewall
Harding was ordained as pastor of the new
society upon condition that, if, at any time two
thirds of the voters should be opposed to his

remaining, he should at the expiration of six months from the time of receiving notice of this, leave the pulpit. After Mr Harding had labored several years in the ministry, the people became somewhat dissatisfied, because he refused to exchange pulpits with the Unitarian clergymen in the neighborhood. On the 4th of April, 1825, the parish held a meeting and the vote was taken in regard to Mr Harding's dismission. There were sixtytwo votes in favor of his being dismissed and fifteen against it. Notice was therefore given to Mr Harding of the wishes of the majority of the parish, and, at the expiration of six months, on the 4th of October, he left the house. But he did not leave the place. This it was supposed by many he was under obligations to do, if governed by a fair and honest construction of the spirit and intention of his contract as understood by both parties at the time it was made. On the contrary he remained and exerted himself to the utmost to divide and destroy the society. He took with him when he left the house his whole church consisting of four or five male members together with quite a number of females, and fourteen members of the parish. When it is said that he took with him his whole church, it must not be understood that these were all in

the society who were interested in the subject
of religion, nor yet all who had made an open
profession of their faith. There were some who
had removed from other places to Waltham,
and who were connected with the churches in
the places from which they had removed.
There were others desirous of making an open
profession of their faith. Both of these classes
were prevented from uniting with Mr Harding's
church because they could not conscientiously
assent to every article in the creed adopted by
that church. Such was the situation of the
society when Mr Whitman began to preach to
them in November, 1825. For the first six
months the congregation did not average one
hundred in number. According to the parish
records there were ninetytwo members, after
the fourteen who went with Mr Harding had
left. The members of the parish had been in
the habit of absenting themselves from public
worship during the latter part of Mr Harding's
ministrations, and it was difficult to break up
this habit. And as Mr Harding had during the
last six months of his stay taken special pains
to warn his hearers against Unitarianism and to
fill their minds with prejudices in regard to
Unitarian preaching, he carried with him a large
number of females, and some of those who did

not go with him were afraid to venture into a
place where, as they had been told, damnable
heresies were to be proclaimed. On the fifteenth
of February, 1826, Mr Whitman was ordained.
The sermon upon this occasion was preached
by his brother, the Rev. N. Whitman, of Billerica. The preacher, in endeavoring to adapt
himself to the peculiar circumstances of the
case, chose for his text, these words, " Hold
fast the form of sound words;" and, in speaking from them, he endeavored to prove by argument that the doctrines now to be preached
in that place, as distinguished from those which
had been preached there before, were the true
doctrines of the Gospel. Thus it will be seen
that Mr Whitman, instead of going to a quiet
and peaceful situation, where he could pursue
his own plans for the improvement of his people
unmolested by those around him, was placed in
the midst of contention. The circumstances
of his situation and the tone of services at his
ordination wore a controversial aspect. As is
usual in such circumstances, the gossip of the
village partook strongly of the spirit of religious
controversy. Scarcely a day passed in which
Mr Whitman did not hear of some new charge
or of some new change rung upon old and oft
refuted charges against Unitarianism. Not-

withstanding his previously formed plans of
quiet devotion to the practical improvement of
his people, he felt that there are times when
such charges should be noticed. He saw that
his own people were in danger of falling into
the belief that charges so confidently asserted
and so boldly maintained might be true or at
least based upon truth. He felt himself called
upon then by the solemn claims of duty to enter
the thorny path of religious controversy. He
learned that the charge most confidently asserted
and most boldly maintained — the charge too,
which at that time and in that place was exerting greater influence than any other to deter
men from examination, was contained in the
assertion, that " *Unitarians denied the Lord
that bought them.*" This assertion he determined at once to notice not merely by denying its truth — not merely by an argument in
proof of his own opinions, but by turning the
charge upon those who made it. Such were the
circumstances and the feelings which gave rise
to his sermon on " Denying the Lord Jesus,"
which was published in August, 1827. This
discourse was based upon those startling words
of our Saviour, " Whosoever shall deny me
before men, him will I also deny before my
Father in heaven."

There was never perhaps a single discourse, an occasional pamphlet, which, to use a bookseller's phrase, had a greater run than this. It went through several editions, which were sold as fast as they could be printed. The argument which it contained in support of Unitarian views of the Saviour was so direct — the steps between the premises and the conclusions were so few and simple and natural — the conclusions themselves were so clearly stated and so well fortified by appropriate quotations from the scriptures, that it took hold of the great mass of the community — while the peculiar form of the discourse was such as to startle the mind, excite thought and call forth inquiry. It shook the faith of many who were before confident in their belief of the opposite doctrines — while it confirmed the faith of those who were hesitating, desiring, and at the same time fearing to adopt the pure and simple and scriptural views of Unitarianism. This discourse produced a great sensation among those whose charges it was intended to repel. They professed to feel sadly grieved to think that they should be accused of denying the Lord, forgetful it is presumed of the frequency with which they had themselves brought this accusation against their brethren, or supposing themselves possessed of the exclusive right to censure and condemn, regardless of the feelings of those who were the subjects of their censure and condemnation. Let it not be supposed that Mr Whitman really intended to bring against his brethren the charge of intentionally denying the Lord that bought them. Nothing could have been farther than this from the promptings of that universal charity, which it was ever his wish to cherish. His discourse was an *argumentum ad hominem*, a turning of the tables upon those who had been for a long time accustomed to bring the charge of denying the Lord with all the gravity of serious accusation against him and those with whom he was connected. It was intended to teach those, whose charges it repelled, a lesson of christian prudence at least, if not of Gospel charity. Mr Whitman was gratified, as every one placed in his peculiar circumstances would have been, with the success of his first attempt.

The next charge which Mr Whitman thought it important to notice, was the charge, then quite prevalent, and still not quite forgotten, that Unitarians do not believe in the necessity of regeneration or a change of heart. He therefore prepared and published a discourse on regeneration. This discourse was printed in

February, 1828. It was well received, but had by no means so great a run, as the one on Denying the Lord. Nor did it produce so great effects as were produced by that. Three editions of this discourse were printed, the two first and a part of the third were sold.

In January, 1828, the Unitarian Advocate was started in Boston. Mr Whitman was actively instrumental and exerted much influence in bringing this publication into existence, and for two years was a frequent contributor to its pages. His articles were always marked with the initials of his name. But had this not been the case, they might at once be known by the peculiarities of their style. One of these articles, a " Sermon on the limited influence of the Gospel," was printed in a pamphlet form and widely circulated.

In December, 1828, Mr Whitman published a Thanksgiving discourse on " The means of increasing public happiness." This discourse expresses fully his views in regard to popular education and the means of promoting it. The ideas expressed are those by which he was himself guided in his efforts for the improvement of his own people.

Mr Whitman found, as it might naturally have been supposed he would, in a society, collected from all parts of the community, many prevalent and, as he thought, debasing superstitions. He therefore selected, as appropriate to a Lyceum Lecture, the subject of " Popular Superstitions." This lecture at once attracted attention and became highly popular. It was delivered, not only in Waltham, but before the Lyceums of several neighboring towns, and in February, 1829, was published.

In June, 1829, Mr Whitman was called upon to preach before the Ancient and Honorable Artillery Company, on their 191st aniversary. The Rev. Mr Pierpont preached the year before, and made, what was regarded at the time, a bold attack upon the whole militia system. This circumstance directed the attention of Mr Whitman to the same subject. He gave his discourse the general title of National Defence, and took occasion to introduce, as one of its topics, a defence of the general features of the militia system. He admitted the existence of evils, but contended that they were not necessarily connected with the system, that they were abuses, which might be removed not only without injury to the system itself but much to its advantage.

In January, 1830, Mr Whitman was called to preach at the ordination of the Rev. Stephen

A. Barnard, over the Church and Congregation in Wilton, N. H. He had for a long time been impressed with a belief that many of the doubts and difficulties upon the subject of religion arose from the want of clear and correct views of the true nature of Christian salvation. He selected this as the subject of his discourse. The sermon was requested for the press by the society before which it was preached, and was printed. The American Unitarian Association then adopted it as one of the first series of their tracts, and in that form it has passed through several editions, and been extensively circulated and generally read.

During the course of this year, Mr Whitman engaged in the publication of a work of an altogether different character from any which he had before attempted. The circumstances which led to this were as follows. Professor Stuart, of the Andover Theological Seminary, addressed two letters upon the subject of religious liberty to Rev. Wm. E. Channing. These letters were called forth, as Professor Stuart himself asserted, by charges, which had been brought against the Orthodox portion of the community in Dr Channing's writings,—charges of hostility against true religious liberty. Mr Whitman was satisfied that these letters of Professor Stuart's were exerting and would continue to exert a vast influence if left unanswered. He ascertained that Dr Channing had no intention of answering them. He therefore prepared, and in December, 1830, published an answer in two letters to Professor Stuart, upon the subject of religious liberty. Professor Stuart had denied the charge, that it was the tendency of orthodox measures to abridge religious liberty. This denial could be met only by an array of facts. This Mr Whitman attempted — and in the attempt he was signally successful. The charge was most fully substantiated by a great variety of well authenticated facts. These letters to Professor Stuart were reviewed in the Spirit of the Pilgrims, a leading orthodox journal, and were thought, by the conductors of that work, of so much importance, that the whole of one number was devoted to the review. This review was answered by Mr Whitman some time during the year 1831. There soon appeared a short letter from E. Pierson, Deacon of Mr Harding's church, in Waltham, addressed to the candid, and purporting to have been called forth by " Whitman's Letters." It was the object of both the review in the Spirit of the Pilgrims and of Deacon Pierson's Letter to the Candid, to convince the commu-

fiity that Mr Whitman had been over credulous
in his collection and careless in his statement of
facts — that he had either given to these facts a
wrong coloring, or had drawn from them unau-
thorized inferences. Mr Whitman, therefore,
both in his answer to the review and in his
reply to Pierson's letter substantiated his assertions by letters, certificates and testimonials
from competent and unimpeachable witnesses.
With the "Reply to Pierson's letter to the Candid," this controversy closed. In regard to the
stand taken by Mr Whitman in this controversy,
it may be remarked that an effort of the kind
was called for. The state of the times — the
dictatorial and denunciatory tone of the Orthodox — and the peculiar circumstances of the
occasion called loudly for such an effort. And
there was never perhaps a man better qualified
to meet exactly and promptly the call which was
made, and to put forth precisely the kind of
effort required, than Mr Whitman. There was
something in his appearance and character
which encouraged the near approach of all with
whom he might casually meet, and inspired
within them a reposing confidence in his willingness to listen to any disclosures which they
might make, and to afford them any assistance
which they might need. Consequently there

9*

was no man in the denomination, it is presumed, who had received so extensive and so minute information in regard to the movements of the orthodox portion of the community. Then there was a quickness of perception in regard to the relation between incidental acts or single measures and the general spirit by which they were prompted—and a retentiveness of memory in regard to casual conversations by which he was enabled to bring together and to apply pointedly the information which he possessed. Indeed he was in every respect just the man to meet the call of the times. He did meet it and perform the task thus providentially assigned him with much credit to himself, and with much profit to the cause of religious liberty. The controversy produced a perceptible effect upon the community. The tone of orthodox denunciation was lowered if not hushed — the bitterness of sectarian animosity was rebuked and somewhat checked.

The year 1831, was distinguished by great exertions on the part of the orthodox, in the promotion of those religious excitements technically called revivals. New measures were adopted. Public religious services were protracted from four to forty days, and the whole orthodox community was thrown into a religious

ferment. Mr Whitman was informed that the
Rev. Mr Harding had made the following statements ; " that these excitements were enjoyed by
none but orthodox denominations, that they
were produced by scriptural means and measures, that they yielded the genuine fruits of the
Gospel, that they were the special work of the
holy spirit, and that all who opposed them were
enemies to the cause of Christ." These statements seemed to Mr Whitman so entirely contrary to the truth that he determined at once to
notice them. He therefore prepared and published a " Letter to an Orthodox Minister on
Revivals of Religion." This letter contains a
satisfactory refutation of the statements of Mr
Harding, and many sound views, together with
much information upon the general subject of
revivals, or religious excitements.

In 1832, Mr Whitman prepared and published
a volume of doctrinal and practical discourses,
to which he gave the title of " Village Sermons."
This volume contains twentytwo short sermons.
It has been extensively read and very generally
liked even by members of different denominations. These sermons possess several important excellences. They are short ; the divisions
are natural and distinct. The arguments are
direct and to the point, and the application is
close and pungent.

But it is in vain to expect that any one publication will meet the views of all. The Village Sermons, though generally approved, called
forth an attack from a Mr Paige, the Universalist minister in Cambridgeport, which appeared
in the Trumpet, a Universalist paper published
in Boston. It was probably this attack, which
led to Mr Whitman's next publication. This
was a volume of letters to a Universalist, which
was published in the spring of 1833. The arguments in these letters are directed against
that peculiarity of modern Universalism, the
rejection of the belief in any future punishment.
It is their object to establish the fact that there
will be a future righteous retribution — without
entering at all upon the inquiry as to the nature
and extent of the punishment that may be inflicted. This volume was prepared under unfavorable circumstances and written in great
haste and without opportunity for re-examination.
Mr Whitman sent to the printer each morning
what he had written during the previous day.
Under these circumstances it will not be thought
strange that the volume should contain some
arguments which are weak or sophistical — and
which the author himself would upon further
reflection have rejected. But even when every
allowance of this kind is made, and everything

weak and not to the purpose is rejected, there are arguments in sufficient number and of sufficient strength remaining to refute the doctrines at which it was aimed, and to establish the positions it was intended to support. The book was never distinctly and formally answered. It was noticed in the Universalist papers; but in such a way as was evidently intended to stifle all interest or curiosity in regard to it.

During the year 1832, Mr Whitman delivered an address at the dedication of the Masonic Temple, Boston — and a sermon on Christian Union at the ordination of Rev. Adin Ballou, in Mendon, Mass. which were published. The one contained a defence of, or rather an apology for Free Masonry — the other the grounds on which Christians of different denominations may unite.

In 1834, Mr Whitman, in connexion with the writer of this memoir, the Rev. Geo. Nichols, and Mr A. P. Peabody, started a monthly publication, called the Unitarian. Before the first number of the work appeared Mr Peabody was ordained over the South Congregational Society in Portsmouth, N. H., and was compelled by the extensive and arduous labors required in a large parish to relinquish his connexion with the work. In February, 1834, the writer of this

Memoir was called from the charge of his parish in Saco, Me., to enter upon the office of
General Secretary of the American Unitarian
Association, and was compelled by the great
responsibilities and various duties of that office,
to relinquish his connexion with the work.
About the same time the Rev. George Nichols
changed his pursuit, and ceased to be associate
editor of the work. The Unitarian was now
published by Munroe and Nichols, and edited
by Mr Whitman. But this arrangement was
scarcely made before Mr Whitman was himself
attacked by that flattering but fatal disease
which terminated in a few months his life of
activity and usefulness. The editorship of the
Unitarian was, during the months of Mr Whitman's sickness, in other hands. The plan of
this publication was a favorite with Mr Whitman. But he was never able fully to develope
his plan. Disappointments in his arrangements
and his own sickness prevented him from making it what he intended to have it, and which
he wished to see it.

The publications of Mr Whitman, which
have here been named, have been for some time
before the community. The opinion of the
public in regard to their character and merits
was probably made up, if not pronounced, as

they successively appeared. The occasions, which called forth most of these publications, have passed away, and the sectarian feelings of partiality or prejudice, with which they were viewed, have subsided. It may be well then to pause in our narrative and dwell for a moment upon his character as a writer. In doing this, it is important that we should know his own views and feelings upon the subject, what he proposed and aimed at in his writings, and why he was led to embrace the peculiar notions which he held upon the subject.

When Unitarian Christianity was first known in this country by that distinctive name, it made its appearance among that portion of the community who were most advanced in a literary point of view. It numbered among its advocates and preachers some of the most finished writers of their time. It boasted of a Freeman, a Buckminster, a Thatcher, and a Channing. These and many others, their fit associates, were men of thought, and they were speaking to men of thought ; they were men of cultivated minds and refined tastes, speaking to men of cultivated minds and refined tastes. They were themselves more interested in and more profited by justness and power of thought when presented in simplicity of style, than by any direct ness of address or earnestness of appeal. Their hearers were for the most part in the same state of feeling with themselves. They were compelled, therefore, from the very circumstances in which they were placed, as well as by their own tastes, to make it their object to think deeply and justly, and to speak with purity and elegance. This circumstance had its effect, both upon the spread of the peculiar sentiments advocated and upon the style of many of those young men who came forward as the heralds of the system. In many places the few, of enlightened views and cultivated minds and refined tastes, had embraced Unitarian Christianity and were interested in Unitarian preaching. The many, who were not particularly interested in beauties of style and who could not in all cases seize upon and appreciate justness of thought unless presented in a fervent and direct manner, were strongly prejudiced against this form of Christianity. It was called a cold, intellectual, philosophical, lifeless system, not calculated to touch the heart or move the soul. This was the charge brought against the system by its opposers, and in many places believed by the great mass of the community. Nay, more, the truth of this charge was in many cases admitted even by the friends of Unitarian Christianity themselves. For some of these, when they looked at the fact that its spread was principally among the more enlightened, began to suspect and to admit that it was a system adapted only to men of elevated minds and refined tastes, and that it ought not to be expected to spread among men of all degrees of intellectual power and of all grades of intellectual improvement.

Then too, the young men, who were preparing for the ministry, naturally looked up with great respect to the most prominent preachers of their own denominations. They did not indeed strive directly and intentionally to imitate. But regarding these as eminently successful and useful in their profession, and knowing that their productions were highly valued on account of their finished literary character, they were led, almost unavoidably, to aim at high literary finish in their own productions. In doing this, there were some who sacrificed directness of address, and lost all earnestness of manner, who, in aiming at the literary excellence, overlooked the moral power of their discourses. They fell into the essay style of writing, and, consequently, lost their influence with a large portion of the community, who were

10

interested in the directness and earnestness of preachers of other denominations.

Mr Whitman was reared, not among the literary or the refined, but among the respectable and intelligent yeomanry, among the people. He had been led to embrace Unitarian Christianity, not in consequence of any cultivation or refinement in himself superior to those around him, not because his attention had been drawn to it by the finished style of its advocates, but because he had found it, as he believed, in the sacred scriptures, and had felt it to be the power of God unto salvation from the love and the influence of sin. He regarded Unitarian Christianity not as an accidental mode, in which the truth of God is presented, and which is adapted only to men in a certain state of intellectual improvement, but as the truth itself, in a good degree of purity, adapted to the human soul and given for the salvation of men of all capacities and all degrees of progress. He had experienced, as he believed, to a certain degree, its regenerating power in his own soul, and, in the true spirit of the Gospel, he wished that every one else might enjoy its influences and share its blessings. It was not associated in his mind with cultivation of intellect, refinement of taste, or beauty of style, as its necessary precursors and companions, and he saw no reason why others, why the great mass of the community might not be made familiar with its truths and experience its power. He aspired to the honor of laying open the glorious truths of the Gospel, as held by Unitarian Christians, to the great mass of his fellow men. Under the influence of this wish, he sought to understand the reason why it had not spread more widely. He soon perceived that, in many minds, the truth itself had been identified with the particular mode and style of presenting this truth, to which the circumstances of the times had given rise.

He perceived too that this confounding the mode of presenting truth with the truth itself, though natural to the great mass of the community, was not an immediate evil,—that the same truth might be presented in various modes. And he felt that there was no reason to conclude that, because men trained up in literary society and to literary pursuits did not speak upon the subject of religion in a style interesting to the great mass of the community, who had been trained up in other scenes and to other pursuits, the particular form of religion embraced by the one class was not adapted to the other.

With these views and feelings he looked at the

community, at their modes of thought and habits of reasoning, as well as at their manner of speaking, that he might ascertain the precise point of the difficulty and learn the best mode of addressing them. He became satisfied, as he looked, that the great mass of the community were not accustomed, in their own mental habits, to long processes of reasoning, and were, consequently, unable to follow such processes when listening to others. Often, has the writer received from the subject of this memoir the following advice in regard to argumentative discourses. " Make your premises perfectly clear and distinct, and let your statement of them be as brief as may be consistent with perspicuity. Then be particular to have but a few steps, and those short, obvious and direct, between your premises and your conclusion. If you have many steps, a long process of reasoning, your hearers will lose sight of your premises before they arrive at your conclusion, their minds will become confused, their interest will flag, and no impression will be made, no conviction produced. This, he added, he had often observed in congregations where the opposite course had been pursued. The hearers would be all attention at first, but would, one after another, lose their interest, as they became unable to follow

the extended process of reasoning." This advice embodies one of the maxims or principles
which Mr Whitman had adopted as the guide
of his own efforts in argument. *" The premises
clear, distinct and intelligible; the steps between
the premises and the conclusion few, direct, natural and short."*

Again, he became satisfied that the great
mass of the community were not accustomed to
abstract courses of reasoning; but were in the
habit of reasoning in particulars, by dwelling
upon and following out individual cases. He
noticed that, when men of business stated an
abstract conclusion as a general principle, they
almost always referred for support of the correctness of that conclusion to individual cases,
either real or supposed. He noticed, still further, that, when an abstract conclusion was
stated to such and they wished to examine its
correctness, they asked how it would apply in
individual cases, shewing, as Mr Whitman
thought, that their processes of reasoning were
conducted by dwelling upon individual cases,
although their conclusions might be general and
abstract. From this circumstance, he was led
to think much of the importance of illustrations.
His advice upon this point was, " You may pursue one of two courses. You may state your

abstract principle or conclusion and then bring
forward an individual case in illustration of
your principle and of the process by which you
arrived at your conclusion. Or you may take
an individual case and follow it out, until your
hearer is led along with you to your conclusion.
But, whatever may be the order of arrangement
which you may adopt, you will in all cases succeed best in interesting your hearers, by presenting a subject in detail and with the illustration of particular cases and examples." This
advice, like that last noticed, embodies the principle which he had adopted as the guide of his
own efforts. Perhaps the principle may be
better understood and more fully appreciated if
an example be added. From the fourth page of
his tract upon Christian Salvation, the following
paragraph is selected, as illustrating the manner
in which Mr Whitman himself carried out this
principle.

I. "What, then, is christian salvation? It
is deliverance from ignorance, error and sin, —
and the possession of christian knowledge, virtue and piety. Perhaps I can render this defini-
tion more clear by a familiar example. Suppose
then that a learned heathen now stood before
me; one who worshipped idols, — one who had
heard of Jesus, and believed him to be an im-

postor, one whose conduct was openly immoral.
I undertake to convert him to Christianity by
rational argument and evangelical motives. I
first convince him of the existence of one infinite Creator, Governor and Father. You perceive that he would then be saved from his ignorance concerning the nature and perfections of
the Supreme Being ; as well as from the folly and
darkness of idolatry. I next convince him that
Jesus of Nazareth is the divinely commissioned
Saviour of the world. You perceive that he
would then be saved from his erroneous opinions
respecting the one Mediator between God and
men, as well as from an evil heart of unbelief.
I further convince him that if he be a true
Christian he must obey the instructions, imitate
the example and imbibe the spirit of the Great
Author and Finisher of our faith. When his
actions give evidence of a reformation of heart
and life, you perceive that he would be saved
from his iniquities as well as blessed with a
righteous and holy character. When these
things are accomplished you must admit that he
has experienced christian salvation.

" Now from this illustration, you may learn
four most important Gospel truths. First, that
christian salvation consists in deliverance from
ignorance, error and sin, and in the possession

of christian knowledge, virtue and piety. Secondly, that this salvation takes place whenever
a person becomes a practical Christian. Third-
ly, that so long as any one continues a practical
Christian, he is in no danger of punishment.
And fourthly, that divine pardon can be obtained only by forming a christian character."
In this example it will be seen that Mr Whitman first states his general position. He then
takes an individual supposed case, and conducts
his reasoning process by dwelling upon that,
until he leads his hearers along to the general
conclusion which he had at first stated. This
then was the second principle at which Mr
Whitman, in his examination of the modes of
reasoning prevalent in the community, had
arrived.

Still further, he was satisfied that it was important, in addressing an argument to the community, to make the points and different steps in
that argument perfectly clear and distinct and
separate from each other. He regarded many
discourses as general herangues upon the subject, of which they treated. There was, indeed, a course of argument perfectly clear to
the mind of the speaker, but the points and
steps in that argument were not made clear to
the hearer. Consequently, the hearer met

with no resting places; but found his attention taxed from beginning to end. This he observed was different in the arguments of lawyers at the bar. They addressed men, not for the purpose of saying eloquent things upon the subject before them, but for the purpose of convincing them of the truth of certain positions and leading them to act according to their convictions. He noticed that they endeavored to make one point clear and distinct and to sum up their arguments in its support, before they passed to a second. In this way he observed that the minds of hearers might be intensely taxed by the arguments in support of any particular point. Because, when these arguments were summed up, the point was dismissed from their mind as settled, they were permitted to relax their attention, rest for a moment and prepare for the examination of a second point. Mr Whitman, therefore, adopted this as another principle for his own guidance in the management of an argument, " to have the several points or steps in his argument clear, distinct and separate from each other, and the arguments in support of each point carefully summed up before passing to a succeeding point. An extract from his Tract on Christian Salvation, will serve to illustrate both this and the principle first noticed, that of having the steps between the premises and the conclusion few and direct and short. "I am secondly, to prove that this salvation takes place whenever a person becomes a practical Christian. Look again at the argument from revelation." (This had been referred to in support of his first point.) "What did Jesus say to the penitent female who anointed his feet at the house of Simon the Pharisee? ' Thy faith hath saved thee ; go in peace.' *Hath saved thee;* not will save thee at some future period ; but, hath even now secured thy salvation. His miraculous powers enabled him to know that her repentance was sincere, that her reformation was commenced, that her belief in his divine mission would influence her to strive for christian perfection. What is the exhortation of Paul to his beloved Timothy? ' Be thou partaker of the afflictions of the Gospel, according to the power of God, who hath saved us.' *He saved us.* If he had before saved them, their salvation could not be an event of futurity. The same apostle makes these explicit declarations to his apostles. ' We are saved by hope.' ' By grace ye are saved.' *Are saved.* In both cases the salvation was then experienced. This meaning is more strongly expressed in the original. The literal translation is this, we *were* saved by hope — by grace ye *were* saved. Thus no doubt remains that he spoke of an event already passed. Take one example from the epistle of Peter. 'The like figure whereunto even baptism doth now save us.' *Doth now save us.* This ordinance was then leading them to the acquisition of christian knowledge, virtue and piety, and thus saving them from ignorance, error and sin. If then our Saviour pronounced his disciples saved, as soon as they cordially embraced his religion; and if the inspired apostles declared that their reformed converts, as well as themselves, had already experienced salvation; surely Christian Salvation takes place whenever a person becomes a practical Christian." This extract illustrates, to a certain degree, the principle of which we are speaking. He had already stated and argued his first point, that Christian salvation consists in deliverance from ignorance, error and sin. He had summed up his arguments and closed his remarks upon the point. That was put down in the mind of his hearers as settled. They had rested their minds from the attention with which they had been taxed, and were now prepared to listen with renewed attention to the second point and the arguments that might be alleged in its support. The advantages which he expected from this mode of argument were, that he secured a closer and more undivided attention to each particular point and the arguments in its support; could keep up the attention for a longer time, by means of the rests thus afforded; and could so present his arguments, that they could be more readily retained and carried away and more easily examined and estimated.

Finally, he was satisfied that many discourses from the pulpit, and especially, many occasional discourses, failed of interesting the assemblies to which they were addressed, because those who prepared them, consulted in the preparation their own tastes and states of mind, rather than the circumstances of their hearers. When requested to preach on any particular occasion his feelings were, " I have an opportunity of speaking to this people, and for once only perhaps in my life. What are the peculiar circumstances of the people, on what are their minds now awake, to what is their attention now directed, on what subject do they most need information, in regard to what point do they most need to be aroused?" The answers to these questions determined his selection of subjects for his occasional discourses.

The general principles, in regard to writing,

which **Mr** Whitman had voluntarily adopted
and distinctly avowed, have now been stated.
He wished to be, and was regarded as, a
plain writer, a writer for the people — the
great mass, the less informed. Much is often
said of the importance and the means of coming down to the comprehension of the people.
And many, in attempting this, begin by simpli-
fying their language. In doing this they give
to the people what others would call *baby talk*,
which always fails of its object, and, in most
cases, proves disgusting. Mr Whitman's ideas
of coming down to the comprehension of the
unlearned were altogether different from these.
He never troubled himself about his language.
Almost the only expressions ever heard by
the writer from him as to mere language,
were in regard to the importance of seeking for
purity and simplicity of language. His advice
referred to other points. Be particular to acquire yourself, in the first place, clear and distinct ideas upon the subject on which you are
to write, in all its parts and branches. Then,
in preparing to present the subject to your
hearers, be careful to arrange your points in a
natural order, so that the one may almost unavoidably lead on to the other, and the mind of
your hearers may be led along step by step to

11

your conclusion, his interest becoming greater at every successive step of his progress. Still further, select those arguments and proofs in support of your several points, which are most direct and to the point and which can be most briefly stated. And finally, seek out familiar and appropriate illustrations. Such were Mr Whitman's views of the way of coming down to the comprehension of the people. Whether in his writings he carried out these views is, a question which must be left for his readers to determine.

In addition to these general principles, there were certain peculiar tastes, for which Mr Whitman could not himself account; but which he admitted had an influence upon his style of writing. The most important of these was an inherent love of proportion in the parts of a discourse. If, for example, his discourse should be divided into three distinct heads, he was strongly prompted by this feeling to make these several heads, if possible, of equal length, and even of an equal number of paragraphs. If a discourse should be divided into three general divisions, and the first of these divisions should contain three subdivisions, he would labor to have each general division contain the same number of subdivisions and to have each subdi-

vision of about the same length, Or, to take
an example from his published writings. In the
Unitarian he published a letter to Trinitarians,
giving a certain number of reasons why. he
had been led to reject the doctrine of the Trinity. In the next letter he gave the same number of reasons for embracing the doctrine of
the divine unity. In the last letter the divisions
are made, not as dictated by the nature of the
case, but that they might correspond with the
numbers of the preceding letter. A careful
observer will notice the influence of this feeling
continually manifesting itself in his published
writings. It was a feeling of which he often
spoke to the writer, but which he did not attempt to defend, regarding his feelings in this
respect simply as a matter of taste.

It has been suggested by some that, as there
was the appearance of freedom, ease and directness in Mr Whitman's writings, they must have
been thrown off without much thought or preparation; that they appear very much as we
should suppose he would converse upon the
same subjects. It is true there is about them
something of that freedom and directness,
which characterize earnest and dignified conversation. But it is not true that they, were
thrown off without thought or preparation. Mr

Whitman's idea of preaching, both in regard to
the structure of sentences and the manner of de-
livery, was, that it should *approach* as near as possible to free, dignified earnest conversation. But
it would have been much easier for him, at first,
to have written in the abstract, general, essay
or dissertation style, than it was to write in the
style which he adopted. The sermon on Denying the Lord, the first of his published writings,
was written over and over again. His course
was, to take each paragraph and write it over
and over until he was himself satisfied, endeavoring at each revision to make it more concise,
clear, simple and direct. And it was in this
way that most of his earlier publications were
prepared. He would undoubtedly have been a
more beautiful writer, had he followed his natural inclination rather than his sense of duty.
But he was writing for a certain purpose, and,
without consulting his own taste or his reputation as a writer, he at once addressed himself
to the accomplishment of his purpose, and labored indefatigably until success crowned his
efforts.

His manner of preparing a discourse for the
pulpit was, as he himself often asserted, to place
before him, in imagination, a young person of
from twelve to fourteen or sixteen years of age,

a well educated bright and intelligent lad, and then, to suppose himself addressing in earnest and dignified conversation this lad, with the intention of so setting the subject under consideration before him, as to produce in his mind deep conviction, and strong interest. For he felt that if he could succeed in reaching the heart and interesting the feelings and influencing the mind of such an one, he should be prepared to speak acceptably and profitably to the largest portion of any religious society.

He acquired the habit in the latter part of his life of studying his sermons out, and arranging all the ideas or arguments before he put pen to paper. 'It wou'd often happen that of an evening, when there was free conversation in the room, he would manifest an apparent listlessness, and indifference to what was passing around him, and would seem to be absorbed in thought. When with only his own family, his hands would occasionally move in earnest gesticulation. At such times, as would afterwards appear, he had been engaged in mentally elaborating a discourse, in selecting his arguments and examples for illustration and arranging his points. In consequence of this habit he was during the last few years of his life, a man of apparent leisure to those who might call upon

11*

him, while yet his pen was productive of more than that of almost any other person. For he was engaged in study at all times and in all places, not merely in general study, but in those particular mental investigations and processes which were to aid him in regard to the particular subjects upon which he was writing.

Mr Whitman's principles, tastes and habits as a writer have now been stated. In regard to his character and success it would be indelicate for the writer of this memoir to give an opinion. He may however be permitted to state one or two facts. When Mr Whitman was engaged in the controversy with Professor Stuart, the publications conducted by the Universalist denomination were loud in his praises, as a nervous and powerful writer, while those conducted by the Orthodox congregationalists were very severe upon him, calling him weak and inefficient. But, when his volume of " Letters to a Universalist" appeared, the tone of both classes of journals was changed. The Universalist publications now found him weak and inefficient, while those of the Orthodox denominations were extolling to the skies his directness, vigor and power. May we not conclude, then, that by an eye not blinded by partiality to one's own views he must be regarded as a vigorous and powerful and efficient writer.

That his writings did take hold of the feelings of the great mass of the people, the writer of this memoir discovered in extended travels as General Secretary of the American Unitarian Association by the deep interest everywhere manifested in his health and plans and labors. Those, who had heard but little about the prominent men of the denomination, or who, at least, merely knew them by reputation, seemed to have an acquaintance with Mr Whitman, and to feel deeply interested in everything connected with him, and in every one more or less nearly related to him. Many expressed a great curiosity to see the man, who had dared to speak out so boldly in opposition to a popular Theology and to Orthodox measures. Many anecdotes might be mentioned illustrative of this interest and curiosity, and tending to shew the effect which his writings had produced, and the general influence of his mind upon the community. One may be singled out from the many and inserted. " Two women were travelling through Waltham, in a chaise. They inquired where Mr Whitman lived. On being directed to the house, they stopped, got out, tied their horse and knocked at the door. Mr W. went himself to the door. They asked if Mr W. was at home. ' Yes,' was the reply —

' walk in.' When they were seated, supposing they had business with him, he said, ' I am Mr W.' ' Are you l indeed!' was the reply. ' Well, we have been reading your books for a long time, and, as we were going through the place, we thought we would stop and see how you looked.' After some pleasant conversation the ladies took their leave."

The character of Mr Whitman as a preacher has been much misjudged by those who have formed their opinion from his published writings. These are mostly of a controversial character. It has therefore been supposed that he seldom ascended the pulpit, unless girded for battle. This is not true. His general preaching was eminently practical, pungent, direct and earnest. It was but seldom that he prepared a controversial sermon. When he did, he endeavored to make thorough work. His discourses of this character were therefore requested for the press, and appeared before the public. He entered the lists of controversy only from a sense of duty. His habits, tastes and feelings all led him in another direction. He was never fond of dispute or contention in conversation. Indeed, so far was he from this, and so much disposed to pass over, unnoticed, remarks and observations the very opposite of his own sentiments, that he seemed at times almost to 'assent to them. He ever contended that the great object of preaching should be, to press home upon men's hearts and consciences, the plain and simple truths of the Gospel. He admitted, it is true, and he practised upon his admission, that there might be times when it was important to state distinctly, explain clearly, and defend as ably as possible, the peculiar truths by which he was distinguished from other denominations of Christians. But the great purpose, which he ever kept in view, and to the accomplishment of which he directed most of his discourses, was to awaken in men a regard for a few, plain and simple but all powerful truths; and to bring these truths home to the feelings and the conscience, until they should become incorporated with all the principles of action, and should manifest their influence in all the conduct of life. His preaching was then in an eminent degree practical.

It was also direct. When he entered the pulpit, he went not merely in an official capacity, to discharge an appointed duty or to deliver a set and formal discourse. He went as a man, deeply interested in what appeared to him to be all important subjects. He went with all the feelings of a man, as a friend to every individual of his hearers, deeply interested in their highest and best welfare, and strongly desirous of bringing into contact with their hearts the truths and principles by which he felt that his own had been purified and rendered happy. He went not to read an ingenious and labored essay upon truth or error, sin or holiness, obligation, duty or happiness, as mere abstractions, things at a distance from his hearers, to be gazed at and speculated about. He went to speak to them about themselves, their spiritual natures, their capacities for goodness and happiness, their various relations, together with the obligations and duties arising from these relations, their past sinful conduct, their present defective or depraved characters, the means of their rescue from sin and the ground of their future hopes. These were to his mind solemn subjects, requiring much seriousness, much earnestness. But they were subjects of the most momentous concern to each one of his hearers personally, requiring great plainness and directness of speech in his addresses to them. He came at once, therefore, into contact with his hearers. It was, *I* entreat, beseech, exhort, and warn *you.* He spoke with much plainness, but at the same time with great kindness and affection. He often spoke with-

out notes. On such occasions he studied his
discourses, endeavored to make himself acquainted with his subject, and arranged in his
mind and sometimes on paper in the form of a
skeleton his various topics and ideas, but left
the language to be supplied at the time of de-
livery. He was a strennous advocate for the
occasional employment of this mode of preaching,
while he was an equally strenuous advocate for
care and labor in thinking out and preparing
written discourses. His idea was, that it was
better to have one well arranged and carefully
written discourse together with one without
notes, than two ill-digested, ill-arranged and
carelessly written sermons. He thought, too,
that in preaching without notes, one felt more
like a man speaking with men, and would acquire and carry from this mode of preaching
into his written discourses much of directness
of address, familiarity of illustration, and earnestness of appeal.

Mr Whitman's writing and preaching were
marked by such faults as would naturally arise
from his circumstances and his views. The
more prominent of these were want of variety
in the mode of treating subjects and in the arrangement of discourses, and an occasional
want of dignity and purity of expression. If

his volume of Village Sermons be examined, there will be found a great similarity in the form and structure of the different discourses, while in his volume of Letters to a Universalist an occasional expression may be discovered which would offend a delicate taste. In addition to these, there is in his directness of manner, something, which in controversial writings seems expressive of bitterness of feeling. This is the more to be lamented as it gives an entirely wrong impression of the man. For there was never, it is believed, a man who engaged so extensively in controversy and in regard to whom so many severe things were said, who really felt less bitterness and animosity towards his opponents than did Mr Whitman. Such are some of the faults which have been noticed in his writings. But it is believed that, on the whole, it may with truth be said, that he was clear, distinct and vigorous as a writer; plain, practical and direct as a preacher.

Mr Whitman's exertions for the good of his people were not confined to the pulpit. He was indeed indefatigable there. But he also looked at their general improvement, and for the promotion of this he put forth his exertions in every possible direction. An idea of these exertions and of the success which attended

them may be obtained from the following testimonials of persons, who were then members of
his parish. One writes thus ; " From the time
of Mr W.'s coming into the place to the day of
his death, he evinced great interest in the cause
of education and in the improvement of the
young. From his having been himself formerly
employed in a Factory, he knew the wants
peculiar to such places. During the spring following his ordination, he proposed to the females
of his parish, who were connected with the
Factories, to give a course of instruction by
means of lectures on Grammar, Geography and
other important but common branches of education. I think these lectures were given twice
a week, at the school-houses connected with the
upper and lower Factories. A number of the
young women recited to him a long-time afterwards.

In the autumn of 1826, Mr Whitman with a
few of his Parishioners called a meeting to take
into consideration the expediency and propriety
of forming the young men into an association
for Mutual instruction. This was before Lyceums were established. The Mechanics' Institute in Boston, and the Franklin Institute in
Philadelphia were the only Institutions of the
kind at that time known to the originators of

12

the association in Waltham. A committee was
appointed, of which Mr Whitman was one, to
report at an adjourned meeting That Committee reported a constitution, by the first article
of which the Association received the name of
the Rumford Institute. That the Rumford Institute has been the means of doing a vast
deal of good, is a fact that no one in this vicinity
doubts. There have been 321 members, who
have paid their initiation fees. From 200 to
300 ladies' tickets are sold annually. The Institute grew so rapidly, from the first, that no
room was found in the place that would accommodate them. Application was made to
the Boston Manufacturing Company for assistance in the erecting of a suitable building.
This Company, finding that the society had in
view the mental and moral improvement of the
persons connected with their establishment,
with a characteris tic liberality, erected a building at their own expense and rented it to the
Institute, with the condition that the rent should
be expended in the purchase of books for the
society, and should the society at any future
time be dissolved, their library should be left
in the hall, as the property of the Boston Manufacturing Company. In addition to this, the
Boston Manufacturing Company presented the

Institute with a small library, which had previously been purchased for the use of their people.

The Rumford Institute has now a well selected library of over one thousand volumes. They have a small Philosophical and Chemical apparatus for the illustration of subjects brought before them in lectures. There have been regular courses of lectures from the first until the present time, about ten years. The lectures are given once a fortnight from October to April, by the members or by some person procured by the members. More than half the lectures are given by our Mechanics and Manufacturers. Once a fortnight a subject is discussed before the society by the members generally, it being however the especial duty of a Committee, to whom the subject is assigned, to examine it and prepare themseves to speak upon it. The library is opened once a week. Upwards of one hundred volumes are exchanged weekly. And the expectations of the originators of the plan have been fully realized.

Mr Whitman's efforts for the improvement of the young were not confined to the Institute, although he labored continually for this, being called upon to supply all failures in lectures and discussions. He endeavored to raise the standard of common education. — He frequently preached upon the subject. He gave his views

upon it most opportunely, before the agricul-
turists, in an address delivered at Concord
before the "Middlesex Agricultural Society."
These views were afterwards laid before his own
people on Thanksgiving day, and before the
public in his printed "Thanksgiving discourse
on the means of increasing public happiness."
They are contained in the five following pro-
positions. He says, 1st. "In the first place, I
would propose that *all our children receive a
high degree of education.*" 2d. "In the second
place, I would propose that *all our children receive a christian education.*" 3d. "In the third
place, I would propose, that *the Christian Ministry should fulfil the important purpose for
which it was established.*" This purpose, he
proceeds to state, "is to induce men to live sober,
righteous and godly lives, to worship the Father
in spirit and in truth, to love their neighbors
as themselves, and to submit themselves to the
authority of the Son of the most High," to promote in short the prevalence of practical piety
rather than to excite an interest in doctrinal or
controversial theology. 4th. "In the fourth
place, I would propose *that a constant supply of
useful reading be furnished for all the members
of society.*" 5th. "In the fifth place, I would
propose that *associations be formed in every town*

for mutual improvement." Such were Mr
Whitman's views in regard to the general improvement of the community. These views he
endeavored to carry out into practical operation among his own people. And, says the
person before quoted, "That his efforts were
not wholly in vain in this place is manifest from
one or two facts, which may be stated. From
the Town Records it appears that in the year
1825, the year that Mr Whitman was ordained,
the town granted one thousand dollars for
schools. In the year 1834 they granted seven-
teen hundred dollars. The object, for which
Mr Whitman had labored, was here in part
accomplished. And then, too, a yearly high
school was established for the children of the
town, in which they could be fitted for any walk
in life.

Mr Whitman had a large miscellaneous library, which might have been styled a circulating
library, as all his people had free access to it.
He looked upon the information contained in
books as common property, which should be
made as free and should be as universally diffused as the light of the sun or the air which we
breathe.

Mr Whitman soon after he was settled, established a Sunday school, with a library for young

12*

people. To establish this library, he requested, from the pulpit, that persons favorably disposed would send in all their juvenile books, so that what one family had bought and read, might become the property of all. He called also on the people to contribute money, according to their ability, for the purchase of new books. The children and young persons attended the school to recite previously assigned lessons, to hear a lecture or general lesson on some subject from one of the teachers, and to change their books. From fifty to seventyfive dollars have been raised annually, for the Sunday school library. Mr Whitman did not stop to consult his means in the purchase of books for the Sunday school library. He bought all that he thought would be useful and looked afterwards to the parish for the means. The Sunday school library has now nearly one thousand volumes of small books for children and young persons. Mr Whitman used to give a general lesson to the school occasionally, but directed his principal attention to the teachers' meetings."

Another friend and former member of Mr Whitman's society writes thus: "To be particular in regard to the exertions of your late brother in the cause of popular education, would be, to give you a history of the Rumford

Institute, one of the earliest associations of
Mechanics for Mutual Instruction. It may
truly be said' that this society owes its formation
and existence to your late brother Bernard. I
do not mean that he first suggested the idea,.
but he exerted himself with all the weight of his
character and influence to carry forward its first
beginnings, until the society grew and strengthened and took the high rank it now holds.
His efforts were unwearied, always ready to
stand in the gap when lectures were wanted,
always zealous, whenever any labor of body or
mind was required for the promotion of sound
learning among the great mass of the people.

His great and peculiar characteristic was to
infuse his own spirit into others. He breathed
the breath of life into the people around him
and made them living souls. There never
seemed, there never *was*, any *self* in your brother.
In this, lay his great power over others. We all,
who knew him, seemed parts of him and he of
us. There was a glorious energy of character
in him, always directing itself onward with a
high and noble firmness. It gathered to itself
all good within its widely extended atmosphere.
Blessed were those who lived within its influence.

So too of the Sunday school of his society.
There was a peculiarity of character in it,

which spoke of your brother. Though he devoted himself less to this, than to the Institute, yet the zeal, which drew others onward in this school and filled both teachers and taught, was derived mainly from his character and influence and personal exertions.

" His efforts in all things relating to popular education and sound morals, were unceasing, never obtrusive, happily timed, never flagging, unflinching and uncompromising, where truth and duty were to be enforced."

Such were the exertions of Mr Whitman for the general improvement of his people. In regard to parochial visitation, technically so called, he was regarded, by many of his people, as somewhat negligent. There were, however, what appeared to his own mind satisfactory reasons for this apparent negligence. He felt that he was called to high and holy duties, that he had a work to perform, which required all his energies and all his time, and that consequently, he had no time to run about among his people for the mere purpose of gossip, even though it might be religious gossip. The object of parochial visiting he considered to be, the formation of a more intimate and spiritual acquaintance with the people, an acquaintance not merely with their health and worldly prospects, but

with their religious impressions and feelings,
with the states of their minds and hearts, that
so one may be the better able to adapt the instructions of both the parlor and the pulpit to
their peculiar wants. With these views of the
objects of parochial visitation, he looked at the
peculiar situation of his people.

The majority of them were connected with
the Manufacturing establishment, and were employed in their respective occupations during
the whole of the day. He could not therefore
visit them according to his ideas of parochial
visitation, during their working hours. And
when they had closed their labors, for the day,
they were crowded into the boarding houses
connected with the establishment, and were,
consequently, so situated, that he could not see
them under circumstances favorable for free
religious conversation. To meet these peculiar
circumstances, he devoted himself as we have
seen to their general improvement. He still
further cultivated towards them a general acquaintance, manifested by a freedom of intercourse whenever he met them, and then threw
open his doors to all who might wish for a more
intimate acquaintance, or who might desire
free and unreserved conversation upon religious
subjects. And it was the case, that many, es-

pecially of the females employed in the factory,
did spend the latter part of many of their evenings at his house, where they were ever received
with perfect cordiality, and enjoyed the most
free and unreserved conversation upon religious
and other subjects, with both Mr and Mrs
Whitman; conversation calculated to elevate
their tastes, improve their minds and purify
their hearts. It would seem therefore, that,
when the peculiar circumstances of his situation
are taken into consideration, Mr Whitman was
disposed to do all, in regard to parochial visitation, which ought to have been expected of
him. His disposition and his principles upon
the subject were undoubtedly right. Yet it is
true, and must not be disguised, that as he became more and more absorbed in his labors for
the public he was less and less inclined in
feeling to spend his time in parochial visitation.
He began to think that it was his sphere of usefulness and of duty, to write for the public
rather than to visit the families of his parish.
But in this, as in most other similar cases, complaints could not have been justly made by any,
who wished for religous intercourse with their
Pastor. For to such his door was always open
and with such he was always free to converse.
These remarks are made, not for the purpose of

pointing out Mr Whitman as an example in
regard to parochial visiting, but because it is
thought that justice to his character requires,
that the circumstances in which he was placed
and his own views in regard to the duty required by those circumstances should be made
known.

A clergyman's usefulness often depends much
upon the character and influence of his wife.
In this respect, Mr W. was peculiarly blessed.
In the month of December, succeeding his ordination, he was married to Miss Elizabeth Hart-
well Crosby, the eldest daughter of Josiah
Crosby, Esq of Billerica, Mass. With this
lady, he had, for several years, been most intimately acquainted. When he taught a school
in Billerica, she was one of his pupils. She
was also one of the number of young ladies
who composed the society for intellectual and
moral improvement, in which he took so deep
an interest. Soon after he left Billerica, he
commenced, with the consent of her parents, a
correspondence with her. He thus enjoyed
opportunities of becoming thoroughly acquainted
with her character and with her views and feelings upon almost all subjects. The interest,
which he early felt in her as a pupil and a friend,
deepened into that strong and heartfelt attachment which is based upon respect and esteem.

Miss Crosby was early distinguished for the strength of her mental powers and for her desire of intellectual improvement. This strength of mental power was accompanied, in her earliest years, by strong passions. But of these she soon obtained the command, so that even while a school girl she was so mild and amiable in disposition, that, although generally the most distinguished in her several classes, she never incurred the envy or dislike of her school-mates. She was favored with good advantages for the completion of her education in all solid and useful learning, and most faithfully did she improve them.

Miss Crosby early received lasting religious impressions. Her parents were professing Christians. It was their desire and their endeavor to train up their daughter religiously. They wished to see her a practical disciple of Christ. For this they labored, — for this they prayed. Their prayers were answered, and their exertions were crowned with success. — Early in life, she manifested in her conduct the influence of religion upon her heart. She seemed to be filled with love for her heavenly Father, and conscientiously abstained from what she thought to be wrong, and practised what she believed to be right. She, seldom if ever, failed to retire to her chamber at morning and at evening for the perusal of the sacred scriptures and for devout prayer. She endeavored to bring all the various parts of her conduct under complete subjection to religious principle, and to breathe in every act the spirit of Christ, to manifest her christian obedience by a proper government of her appetites and passions, and a faithful performance of all her duties. The fruits of her self-discipline and self-cultivation were manifest to all her acquaintances. She was a peculiar favorite with all, and this, on account of her christian goodness.

Such was the preparation of Miss Crosby in heart and character for the peculiar station she was called to occupy in becoming a clergyman's wife. She sympathised deeply with her husband in all his views of extensive usefulness, and entered with heart and soul into all his plans for the good of his people. She welcomed every one to her house, took them cordially by the hand, and by a certain indescribable something there was about her, she made them feel at once perfectly at home with her. She exerted herself to aid her husband, by spending some time, soon after her marriage, in hearing the young women connected with the Factory recite in Grammar, and other branches. But her efforts to aid her husband were not efforts to take upon herself a portion of his duties; they were efforts to lighten his cares in regard to the family, that so he might have more time for his study and might be more free from distractions while there. And then, by her kind attentions to the people of his parish, by receiving them ever cordially at her house and visiting them familiarly, not as a minister's wife, but as an acquaintance and friend, at their own dwellings, she did much to inspire kindly feelings towards herself and her husband, and to prepare them for a favorable reception of his religious instructions. Still further, she interested herself in all their charitable objects — advising, counselling and cheering them on. Her influence among and over the people of the parish, was the silent but powerful influence of a pure, cheerful, holy life. She won upon their affections by her disinterested and self-sacrificing attentions to them. She secured their respect by an intellectual superiority and moral dignity. She exerted a religious influence over them by manifesting in her own life the power of christian faith and hope and principle to sustain, purify and cheer.

Mrs Whitman became the mother of two sons. The eldest, Josiah Crosby Whitman still lives. The youngest, Bernard, died at about the age of ten months, and but a few weeks before the death of the mother. As a mother, she was most faithful and devoted. She felt that the responsibility during the early years of her children devolved upon her, and she resolutely prepared to meet it. She read much upon the subject of education. She was not one fond of adopting rules laid down by others as of universal application, or of training up her children by book. She had too much sound common sense for this. Nor did she go to the opposite and equally foolish extreme of disregarding all that had been written upon the subject, because she thought it easier to write than to practise. She read upon the subject of education that she might gather hints to aid her in the formation of principles of her own. She was also fond of reading upon the philosophy of the human mind — and of comparing what she read with the testimony of her own consciousness and the results of her observation ; — and she thought that, in this way, she was aided in her preparation for the faithful discharge of the duties of a mother, in her preparation to watch and guide the mental and moral improvement of her children.

Mrs W. had early experience of affliction and

suffering.   Not long before her marriage a sister very near her own age and one with whom
she had enjoyed that most endearing of all intercourse, spiritual communion, in a free and unreserved communication of religious thoughts and
feelings — was taken from her by death.   Then
followed in quick succession, several of her
female friends.   To these succeeded a father —
a most devoted and loving father and two beloved
sisters — who were all borne gradually away by
that most tantalizing of all disorders, the pulmo-
nary consumption.   And about the same time,
her own health began to decline — to manifest
alarming symptoms of the approaches of the
same flattering but fatal disease.   Amid all
these afflictions and sufferings, she was ever
cheerful — so much so as to excite the wonder
of her associates — especially of those who
knew not by experience the sustaining power
of christian faith and christian hopes.   Her
cheerfulness and happy contentment were not
the consequence of a want of sensibility; for
never was there one of more delicate and sensi-
tive feelings, never one more attached as a friend
or affectionate as a relative.   No; her cheerfulness was a moral quality and not a natural
feeling, resulting not so much from constitu-
tional temperament as from religious principle.

For nearly a year after she herself was satisfied that her disorder was really seated upon her, she kept about, and with her usual cordiality she welcomed all visiters and exerted herself to promote their happiness while with her. But at length she found herself too much reduced in strength for these exertions. She therefore withdrew from company and was denied to visiters. This she did, not because it was unpleasant to see her friends, but from a sense of duty, that she might be more quiet and enjoy a better opportunity for religious meditation and reading and prayer. She felt that she was about to take her departure from this world to appear before her God; that her Heavenly Father had, in great love, given her seasonable notice, and that it became her duty to spend the intervening time in preparation of soul for the scenes of eternity. She was able to read but little herself — but she heard much reading from the New Testament and such books of practical and devotional religion as she could obtain. In the latter, she sought for instruction upon one point without satisfaction; and she often expressed her surprise that so little had been written upon the subject of *humility, christian humility.* During her sickness, she conversed with great freedom with her husband upon all

13*

the points of her religious belief — and all the grounds of her christian hopes in regard to a future life.

She was the same during her sickness that she had been when in health — ever cheerful and happy, ever anxious to avoid giving trouble, ever thoughtful of others. Her mind seemed to retain its vigor and elasticity more than could have been expected under so much weakness of body. She manifested great good judgment in the distribution among her friends of such articles as she wished to leave to them, assigning each article to the person to whom it would be most useful. When, a few weeks before her own death, her youngest child died, she was perfectly resigned and even happy in the thought that it had pleased her heavenly Father to take the infant from this world of sin and sorrow, to that world of purity and holiness where she hoped soon to follow.

On the 12th of February, 1831, Mrs W. fell asleep in the gospel hope of a blessed immortality. The circumstances of her death corresponded well with her conduct during sickness. About two o'clock in the morning, she said to her husband, I believe I am dying. He asked her why she thought so ; she answered that she was in great and *peculiar* distress and she thought it must be death. She asked him to feel of her pulse. This he did and told her that it was fluttering. She had read, as many as three times during her sickness, an article in the Christian Examiner on " Erroneous views of death," and was much influenced by what she there read. In accordance with the spirit of that article, she requested her husband not to call the family or disturb their slumbers. She said, on God I depend to sustain me in this hour. Her husband asked her if she still felt happy in the thought of death. She made an effort to speak distinctly and audibly, and said *yes*. She kissed her husband, bid him good bye, saying God bless you. She lay for a few moments quietly and then looked up with a placid smile and said, I did not think I should have breathed so long. A few moments after she spoke so as to be heard by a sister of Mr W. in an adjoining chamber, and said, " Father, into thy hands I commend my spirit." The sister of Mr W. startled by the altered tone in which she uttered these words, was at once by her bedside. She did not speak again, but in a short time quietly fell asleep.

Such was the life, the sickness, the death of Mrs W. A female friend in speaking of her acquaintance with Mr W. says, " I became indebted to him for one of the greatest favors it was possible for him to bestow upon me. He proposed to me a correspondence with his beloved Elizabeth, which we accordingly commenced, and out of it grew one of the sweetest, holiest friendships it has ever been my lot to form and which was interrupted only by her death."

The character of Mrs Whitman and the peculiar circumstances of her sickness and death, have been dwelt upon, in accordance with the design of this memoir, to develope all the various influences to which Mr W. was from time to time subjected. His usefulness it is believed was much promoted by the character and influence of his wife. And from her, too, his own character received a tinge. It is difficult, in a relation so intimate and tender as that of husband and wife, to point out precisely and describe fully the influence exerted by each over the other. And then, too, the influence is reciprocal even in regard to the same traits of character. In the case before us, Mrs W. became acquainted with Mr W. while she was young; she was acquainted with him too as her instructer, and she undoubtedly received an impulse from her husband's character which urged her on to the cultivation of a spirit of entire devo-

tion to duty and of cheerful resignation in affliction. But the circumstance that she became
distinguished for these traits, strengthened and
confirmed the same in her husband's character.
Had she manifested traits the reverse of these,
it is more than probable that her husband's devotion to duty and resignation in affliction would
have been much weakened, if not entirely des-
troyed. But the very sight of his wife amid all
the pains and all the languor of a protracted
disease, and in the full view of the certain and
speedy approach of death — still cheerful —
happy — thoughtful of others, and devoted to
such duties as it was then in her power to perform; this sight must have had, it did have an
influence upon Mr W. in making him resigned,
cheerful and ever devoted to duty. " During
Mrs W.'s sickness, Mr Whitman himself took
much care of her — for the last three weeks of
her life he spent most of his time in the chamber with her, reading to her. He was with her
every night and evinced the greatest degree of
kindness and tender affection — of self-sacrificing devotedness. Yet at the same time he
was cheerful, active and constantly engaged in
his peculiar labors. No one ever heard him
complain of trial or hardship. He took the cup
which Providence gave and drank it bitter and

sweet in the same cheerful, submissive, high-souled temper."

It was the avowed principle of Mr Whitman, that the true Christian should ever " rejoice in the Lord," should bring himself, even in scenes of the most trying affliction, into subjection to gospel principles and christian consolations. He was no stoic, condemning all manifestation of affection or feeling, but he wished to become wholly a Christian, subjecting all his feelings to christian influences and ever regarding the claims of duty as superior to all self-indulgence, even to that melancholy but pleasing self-indulgence, of dwelling upon one's own griefs. He had often expressed to the writer, in conversation, his belief that injury had been done to the christian cause, by the accounts sometimes circulated, of eminent ministers of the gospel who were unfitted for duty and prostrated in their course by overpowering affliction. All such assertions he regarded as a libel upon the sustaining and consoling power of the gospel, or a proof that those concerning whom they are made, were not in all things subjected to 'christian principle. Upon the death of his wife, the practical power of his avowed principles over his own heart and life was put to the test. For a short time after her death, he preferred remaining at home — and while there, seemed absorbed in the contemplation of her character, or if he entered into conversation, which he did even more than he had usually done, with a sister who kept his house, he dwelt upon the virtues and graces manifested by her, whose loss he now mourned. But even at this time, if a neighbor or a friend called, he would carefully avoid obtruding his own feelings upon others, and appeared the same cheerful and happy and kindly attentive man, that he always had done. When, in a short time after the death of his wife, the Review of his Letters to Stuart appeared in the Spirit of the Pilgrims, he at once suppressed his own feelings, and entered with alacrity upon the discharge of his duties to the public, in preparing a Reply to the Review. From this time he seemed to have recovered in a good degree from the effect of this first shock. There was a sobered and saddened grief — but it was mingled with a determined christian cheerfulness, sustained by an active devotion to duty.

In about a year after the death of Mrs W., Mr W. was again married to Miss Sarah Bowers, daughter of Samuel Bowers, Esq. of Billerica, Mass. With Miss Bowers he had long been acquainted, had boarded in her father's family, had corresponded with her, and had been strongly attached to her as a friend. And then too, she was a most intimate and much valued friend of his first wife. A friend she was, with whom they had both enjoyed much spiritual communion, and had arrived at an intimate spiritual acquaintance, and to whom they were religiously attached, notwithstanding Miss B. did, for a time, differ somewhat from them both in religious speculation. In Miss Bowers, he found a worthy successor to his beloved Elizabeth, a devoted wife and an affectionate mother to his son. She still lives to mourn the loss of a devoted and affectionate husband, and to watch with a mother's anxiety over a fatherless child.

Such were the circumstances of Mr Whitman's domestic life. His character here as a husband and a father and as the head of a family manifested the power of christian principles, and showed that with him religion was a living reality, inwrought into the very texture of his soul ; an inward, living spring sending forth a thousand streamlets, and rendering every one who might come within the sphere of its influences more pure and holy and happy.

Mr W.'s labors as a preacher were not confined to his particular charge in Waltham. He was often called upon to engage in a species of

missionary labor. The community, even in the
oldest and most settled parts of New England,
were, to a greater or less degree, in a state of
doubt and even of change upon the subject of
religious opinions. The spirit of the Reformation seemed to be actively at work. It was
thought that the principles adopted by the Reformers had not been carried out to their legitimate extent, and had not produced their proper
results, through a blind devotion to their peculiar
opinions. Consequently, many, acting as they
believed upon the principles and in the true spirit
of the Reformation, were examining into the
religious opinions of the Reformers themselves
and comparing these with the only infallible
standard of religious truth, the sacred Scriptures. In this examination they were led to
reject, in many things, the opinions which had
been adopted by their ancestors and to adopt as
they believed views more scriptural and more in
accordance with those held by the immediate
disciples and early Christians. Those who had
passed through this change in opinions, were
desirous of enjoying religious worship and instruction corresponding with the views they had
adopted — or were anxious that their friends
and neighbors might enjoy an opportunity of
listening to a clear statement, able defence,

and powerful application of these opinions. —
Those clergymen, therefore, who had become
known as the advocates of these more scriptural
views of divine truth, were often called to go
forth to proclaim and defend them and to advise,
counsel, and assist in the organization of religious societies upon their basis.   This was the
case in many of the oldest towns in Massachu-
setts, and where religious societies had for the
longest time been established, as well as in the
newer and more recently settled parts of our
land, where everything seemed unsettled in regard to religious opinions or institutions.   Mr
W. was prominent among those who were thus
called.   And perhaps there was no one more
popular or successful in these labors.   This was
owing in part to the course which he almost uniformly pursued   Others, when they went forth
to this kind of labor, wished to present the practical bearings of their peculiar opinions, and
consequently preached mostly practical discourses based upon them.   Mr W.'s views upon the
subject were these.   These practical bearings,
even, derive their weight in our minds from the
clearness and distinctness with which we behold
the opinions upon which they are based, and
from the firmness of our faith in them as the
truth of God, the truth as it is in Jesus.   And,

consequently, they will lose their influence upon the minds in which there is indistinctness and confusion in regard to the opinions themselves, and some doubt, even, as to their truth. These people, he would say, have long been accustomed to different views of divine truth. They have heard the same christian practices, which you enforce, urged again and again. You, it is true, urge them from different motives, motives which cannot be drawn from the views which they have been accustomed to hear, and motives, too, which to your mind, are all powerful. But their power on your mind is derived from the distinctness of your vision and the strength of your faith in regard to the peculiar opinions from which they are drawn. In order, therefore, that your practical exhortations may come home to the hearts of your hearers, with all the power with which they bear upon your own mind, you must place them in the same situation with yourselves, must make their vision as clear and their faith as strong as your own, in regard to these peculiar opinions. When, therefore, he went forth into the places alluded to, his feeling was, these persons wish to know distinctly and definitely in what respect Unitarians, so called, are peculiar, — what opinions prevalent in the community they have rejected, and the reasons why they have rejected them, — what opinions differing from these they have adopted and the reasons why they have adopted them.   He therefore usually in such labors gave in one discourse — a long discourse, a distinct but brief statement of the prevalent opinions which he rejected, with his reasons for rejecting them, and of his own peculiar views upon the same points, with his reasons in their support. It was a remark often made, after Mr W. had preached at one of these newly formed societies, we have heard Unitarian preachers for several Sabbaths, but never before have we learned distinctly what Unitarians believed, nor the grounds of their belief.   This single discourse, which Mr W. generally preached without notes, he regarded as but an imperfect sketch, and where he had time, he was prepared with written discourses, to enter into a lengthened argument upon each of the points in controversy between Unitarians and others.   Indeed, Mr W. thought it of the utmost importance at the present day, as at all times, that all clergymen in all situations should present to their people clear and distinct exhibitions of their own peculiar opinions and direct and able arguments in their defence.

This he regarded as one of the best means in

the present fluctuating state of the religious community, of binding together the members of a religious society, and thus sustaining religious institutions. Your people, he would say, may be interested in religion, but if it is an interest in it, only as a matter of feeling, others may manifest and excite more feeling than you and may draw them away and thus may do something towards rendering them unsettled and fluctuating in regard to the support of religious institutions. If they are attached to you personally as their minister, they may upon your death be scattered. The only bond of permanent union is an attachment to certain opinions and principles distinctly defined in their own minds, embraced by them with a living faith, opinions and principles cherished in their hearts as the life of piety in their souls and of holiness in their characters.

The different places in New England which Mr Whitman visited as a Missionary, are too numerous to be specified. There are, however, two of which distinct mention may be made. Bangor, Me. and Hartford, Conn. In Bangor, he excited great interest and it was thought did much good. Many of the society were extremely desirous to have him as their Pastor. In Hartford, also he excited great interest, and

14*

great opposition.   On one occasion he was met,
as he came from the stand from which he had
spoken, by a lady who at once commenced an
attack upon his views.   He pleasantly reminded
her that that was no place for religious discussion, and intimated his willingness to meet her at
her own house on the succeeding day.   This he
did, and with each a Bible in hand they spent
some time in earnest but kindly conducted religious discussion.   On another occasion, as he
was walking the streets on the morning after he
had delivered his lecture on revivals he saw that
he attracted much notice.   Many were peeping
to get a sight of him, and he overheard one exclaim, "I know not what we may not expect
next.   There is nothing beyond but Fanny
Wright."

Mr Whitman was called to visit the South,
and the great Valley of the West.   At Cincinnati he preached the sermon at the Dedication
of the Unitarian Church, and supplied the pulpit for several Sabbaths.   He also supplied the
pulpit for several Sabbaths in Louisville, Ken-
tucky.   In Cincinnati, he excited a very deep
and particular interest, and an invitation was
given him to take charge of the new society.   At
Louisville also it is believed that his preaching
was acceptable.   The time spent by him in the

Valley of the West, was not idly wasted. He
went out from Cincinnati, to Dayton and several òther places, and availed himself of every
opportunity to preach. He also spent some
weeks at Richmond, and preached the sermon
at the dedication of the new house in that place.
There, as in some other places, his labors were
acceptable and successful, and he excited among
all with whom he mingled a deep interest in himself personally, as well as in his peculiar views
of religious truth. The late Judge Marshall,
though differing from Mr Whitman in religious
belief, was occasionally his hearer, while at
Richmond, and expressed himself in terms of
high respect for him as a man of sound and log-
ical mind, clear, distinct and able in argument.
A clerical friend somewhat acquainted with his
labors as a Missionary, writes as follows : " He
was eminently qualified to do the work of a missionary. His social qualities and kind feelings
soon attached people to him and gained their
confidence. His manner of speaking upon religious subjects, whether in public or in private,
his earnestness, shewing that he felt deeply what
he said, and regarded religion as the one thing
needful, his sincerity, speaking in every word
and look as ' an Israelite indeed,' and the clearness of his reasoning, carrying conviction often

even to the minds of the prejudiced, all conspired to make him successful in his missionary labors. His power of convincing men of the truth and importance of what he taught was remarkable. His reasoning was direct and conclusive and it was difficult for his hearers not to be affected by it. A few years before his death, I travelled with him in the Western States. He preached at Cincinnati, Ohio, Louisville, Ky., and at several other places, and always to full houses. He made a deep impression on the minds of all who heard him, and he will long be remembered with respect and gratitude by the people of the West. At the South too, particularly at Richmond, Va., he attracted large audiences and was greatly admired by all who heard him. While preaching there he was repeatedly called upon to explain and defend his views of religious truth. He rejoiced in every such opportunity and always did it to the great satisfaction of all who heard him. In one instance a young man, with more of confidence than discretion, violently assailed him before a room full of people. But he was soon convinced of his folly and was covered with shame and confusion. The calm and courteous manner in which Mr Whitman replied to him, together with his clear reasoning and overwhelming arguments, commanded the deepest respect of all present. The Richmond people spoke of him in terms of the highest commendation, and appeared to lament his death as that of an endeared friend and distinguished benefactor."

Mr Whitman possessed to an unusual degree the missionary spirit. His own views were to him dear and valuable, for he regarded them as the truth of God, and he felt them to be the sources of spiritual life. He felt too that he had received them upon trust, for the good of others, and he was willing to labor, to spend time, to put forth exertions, that so he might promote the spread of these views. He often wondered that any christian minister should be devoid of the missionary spirit. And he has often said to the writer, if the ministers in New England would but leave their societies and comfortable homes for a time, and travel and preach in the regions of the far West, they would all return with hearts filled with the missionary spirit.

Mr Whitman's missionary spirit was not confined, in its manifestations, to direct missionary efforts. He availed himself of every opportunity to encourage others to enter upon the work of the Christian Ministry. It is often the case, that young men, who are looking forward with ardent desires but trembling hearts to the christian ministry, are discouraged by hearing the clergymen, with whom they may meet, dwelling much upon their trials and labors. And then too, it often happens that those, who are just about entering upon the profession, are taken by the hand, and when they are expecting some word of kind encouragement or a hearty welcome to the joys of the work, hear only some mournful expression of pity, that they are entering a field of labor, where so much effort is required and so many troubles and disappoint. ments to be encountered. Is there not reason to fear that the silent influence of many clergy- men tends, in this way, to deter from the work of the ministry, some, who, under other circum- stances, would have gladly devoted themselves heart and soul to its labors. Mr Whitman, it is true, regarded the Ministry as a sphere requiring great effort, but then he knew too, that nothing great or worthy can be accomplished without effort. He knew that the ministry had its trials and disappointments and discouragements, but he knew too, that no sphere of labor was without these. He never, in his general conversation or in his intercourse with his ministering brethren, dwelt upon his labors or his trials. If any one thought that Mr Whitman's labors were severe, it was because the results of severe labor were witnessed, and not because Mr Whitman himself ever alluded to their severity. On the contrary, he was more inclined to speak of plans for still greater efforts and still more extensive usefulness, which were in his mind. The influence of his conversation, even the most casual conversation into which he might fall, was to impress the mind with the thought that the christian ministry was not only a great but a glorious work, and to excite an ardent zeal to be pressing forward in this great work. Such was the general tendency of his conversation. Still further, he was ever watchful of the young men with whom he might casually meet, carefully studying their feelings upon the subject of religion, as manifested in general conversation. And his observation was directed to the point, to ascertain, if possible, whether their interest in Christianity, their personal religious and moral character, and their general qualifications of mind and speech were such as to render it proper to counsel and encourage them to enter the christian ministry. The writer well remembers being at Waltham, when a young, now a successful minister of the Gospel, called and was introduced to Mr Whitman, for the purpose of obtaining, through him, of the Middle-

sex Bible Society, some copies of the New
Testament, for a Sunday school in the village
where he then resided.   Mr Whitman, as usual,
so treated him as to make him feel at once apparently most perfectly at home, and entered into such general conversation as to ascertain that
the young man was deeply interested in the
truths of our religion, and, in the true spirit of
this religion, was ardently desirous of extending
these truths far and wide. After the young man
left, Mr Whitman said, I must see that young
man again, he must be advised and encouraged
to enter the ministry.   He has the right kind of
interest in the subject and seems to possess the
right feelings.   All he wants is encouragement
to induce him to devote himself to the work.
And it was in this way, that he was ever upon
the watch ; ready, if he saw one who needed
only a word of encouragement, kindly to drop
it in his ear ; if he saw one, who needed assistance as well as encouragement, faithfully to
render him the assistance he might need.   And
then too, when he met with one who was wishing and hoping, but scarcely daring to resolve
to enter the ministry, most cordially did he take
him by the hand, most kindly did he cheer and
encourage his trembling heart ; most readily
did he offer such assistance as it might be in his

power to give. Nor was this mere profession.
He was ever faithful in his counsel and advice
to those who were preparing for or had entered
upon the ministry.

But perhaps his character in this respect may
be best gathered from the testimony of one,
who experienced his kind encouragement. He
writes thus : " My recollections of your lamented brother, I cannot now express in language worthy the subject or adequate to my
feelings I think of him now, as one of the
company of God's faithful servants, who have
gone to join the glorified spirits of the just ;
and it seems almost a species of sacrilege to
draw down his image, that I may be just in
speaking of what he was when I knew him
here. The spirit now in heaven, was indeed
nurtured here on earth. But oh, what a change
of objects and employments before it there, and
what progress may we suppose it to have already
made since it left this world. How unsuited to
its present character, is the representation of
what it *was* amid the temptations of youth and
the cares and trials of mature age. The good
man here has become the Saint in Heaven.

" Of the point in your brother's character to
which you direct my thoughts, I have often
spoken with great satisfaction, both before and

since his death. I know not one among our
brethren, who ever seemed to feel a stronger
and more hearty interest than he in the character and usefulness of young men preparing for
the ministry. When about to engage in this
work myself, I accidentally met him in Boston,
and in the language of confiding friendship told
him my views and purposes and spoke of the
apparent difficulties I apprehended. I shall
never forget with what earnestness he replied to
me, expressing the deepest interest in my purpose, — obviating the difficulties I apprehended,
entreating me to persevere, and assuring me
that, if no one else gave me encouragement, I
should not rely upon his sympathies and aid in
vain. It was the effect of this expression of
sympathy and promise of countenance and aid
which, more perhaps than anything else, induced me to enter immediately upon the accomplishment of my purposes. Nor did your
brother's kindness cease here. As soon as an
opportunity occurred, after I commenced preaching, I exchanged with him, and then he gave
me a new proof of his faithfulness and regard.
Immediately after my return from Waltham, I
received a long and affectionate letter from him,
in which he plainly pointed out the faults of my
manner of preaching and of my sermons, which

had been observed by those of his parishioners
in whose judgment he had the most confidence,
and gave me such advice and exhortation as
must have proceeded from a heart deeply interested in the cause of religion and the success of
its ministers.   I have always felt that I owed
much to your brother at this and at subsequent
periods of my ministry. And I know that I am
not alone in this consciousness of great obligations to him.   I am persuaded that your brother
was wont to attach much more importance than
is common to those casual connexions which
are formed in our progress through life.   He
felt that important obligations sprung from them,
which he was desirous to fulfil to the utmost.   I
may illustrate what I mean by the instance of
his treatment of myself.   We had met, and, for
a short time, lived together as school-fellows.
But there was considerable disparity in our ages,
enough to prevent that kind of intercourse and
attachment which is common to school-mates of
nearly the same age.   Still I believe that while
he lived he felt himself bound to me by strong
ties of *duty*, and that he never lost an opportunity to inquire after my welfare or to promote
my usefulness.   He loved and labored for his
race, but amidst all his cares and labors for the
good, he never lost sight of any one of

those, with whom he had been, in any way, connected long enough to acquire the power of exerting an influence over them by his precepts or his example. He never ceased to use his influence for their good, even when the changes of life had long severed his connexion with them. I often hear the same testimony from those with whom we were mutually connected at school and elsewhere. And this point in his character seems to me to be one of great excellence. It speaks well for the tenderness of his conscience, and the sensibility of his heart. If it were more common, how would life be disarmed of many of its dangers to the young and the friendless, and of many of its sorrows to the aged and infirm. God does not bring us together in any of the walks of life without a purpose. And I cannot think it too much to say that we should feel and act as if this purpose was not wholly accomplished, while an opportunity remains to do each other good, even though the outward bonds of our connexion be dissolved."

In his zeal to increase the number of laborers in the vineyard of the Lord, Mr Whitman took some steps, which were regarded by many as of doubtful utility. He thought much of the importance of a thorough education as preparatory

to the work of the ministry, and he ever eucour-
aged those; who enjoyed opportunity and means,
to go regularly through a complete course of
preparatory studies. But at the same time he
regarded other qualifications as of more importance than even a thorough course of study.
He looked upon personal piety, devotedness to
the cause, a knowledge of human nature, and a
power of adapting one's self to the peculiar
states and wants of the community, as of the
first importance. He was always rejoiced to see
these united with deep science and extensive
learning, upon all the various important, minute
or critical points of theology. But, if the two
classes of qualities must be separated, he preferred, in a parish minister, the former to the
latter class. In many instances, therefore, he
encouraged individuals, who were somewhat
advanced and who were in indigent circumstances, to adopt a shorter course of preparatory
study. And he was, in this way, instrumental
in introducing into the ministry several, who
had not enjoyed the advantages of a thorough
classical or a regular theological education.

In doing this, he encouraged and assisted
some who were Restorationists in sentiment to
prepare for and enter the ministry. He was not
himself a Restorationist in the proper sense of

15*

that term. He believed the punishment of God, or the consequences of sin, both in this world and in the world to come, to be disciplinary, tending to reclaim the sinful. He believed too that in the future world, as well as in the present, men would be free agents. And he *hoped* that, being free agents, all would finally be reclaimed through the power of Gospel truth, the influences of God's Spirit, and the disciplinary inflictions of his paternal love. But he did not, as do the Restorationists, feel himself authorized to proclaim it to men as a revealed truth that all would finally be restored. He did not consider himself commissioned, as an ambassador of Christ, to declare this doctrine, while, at the same time, he felt that, as a christian philosopher, he might be permitted to indulge the hope that it would prove true. Still he was not bigoted or exclusive in regard to his own speculations, and therefore he did assist some, whom he regarded as giving promise of usefulness in the profession, although Restorationist in sentiment, to prepare for the work of the Gospel Ministry. He also exchanged pulpits with some of this class and took part in the services of their ordination. There were others, and some of them among the most prominent of the clergy, who adopted the same course. Yet there were some, who had strong doubts of the utility of these steps. It seems, from a rough sketch found among his papers, that some one of the latter number had remonstrated with him in regard to his course in this particular, and that he was preparing an answer in defence of his course. But perhaps the true state of the case may be learned from the sketch itself, which though rough and unfinished is here subjoined. It is entitled, " A Letter to a Unitarian Clergyman."

" My Dear Sir, — At our last interview, you expressed to me, in a very christian-like manner, your ' serious fears ' at the course I have pursued in relation to the introduction of men into the Ministry, destitute of a liberal education. The expression of serious fear by one of so high standing, made in so christian-like a manner, I feel bound to notice. I have, therefore, concluded to state the facts of the case and give you the honest reasons of my conduct. The facts are these. I have assisted in introducing into the ministry five individuals of the Restorationist denomination. In two cases I preached the discourse, in one gave the right hand of fellowship in one; made the address to the people; and in one offered the concluding prayer. I have exchanged freely with this class of preachers. I have now studying under my in-struction two in this place and one in another, who have always been called Unitarians, but who are persons of no liberal education. *And I am doing all that I can to induce other good men to devote themselves to this work.* These are the facts. The reasons of my conduct naturally divide themselves into two parts. I. Union with Restorationists. 1st, They are Christians. 2d, They are Protestants. 3d, Consistency requires it. 4th, It is the part of Liberality.

" II. Introduction of uneducated men into the Ministry. I admit that the more learning the better. But something more essential. The various qualities which go to make up what we should call an adaptation to the ministry. Whoever understands the Gospel may preach it. Certain qualifications. Best men for many places, because plain in their manner of preaching, ardent, have entered upon the work from their interest in the success of religion and not because they have got through college and must have a profession, and having been at but little expense for an education, can settle upon smaller salaries."—This it will be seen is but a collection of topics preparatory to a full and labored defence of his course. We can now only lament that he was prevented from giving it to the public, as it might and probably would have contained important views upon the subjects of liberty, charity and christian union, as well as upon the qualifications requisite for the Christian Ministry.

When one looks at the labors of Mr Whitman, at what he actually accomplished, he will be surprised to learn that his sketches and plans of works to be written far out numbered all his actual productions. He never seemed to stop and dwell upon what he had accomplished. He was ever directing his thoughts and earnest inquiries to the wants of the community, and to the sketching of plans to meet and supply those wants. Nor did he confine his thoughts to any one particular class of wants. To give an idea of his character in this respect, it will be sufficient to lay before the reader a detail of some of his plans and sketches, as known to the writer or found among Mr. Whitman's papers.

1. He had, as has been already hinted in another part of this memoir, sketched a plan of a volume of letters to College Students, to be filled up by himself and the writer of this in connexion.

2. He had also sketched a plan of a volume upon the doctrines of our religion, a sort of doctrinal guide, to be filled up in the same way.

3. There appears among his papers a sketched plan of a volume of letters on Domestic Happiness, entitled " *The Wedding Present.*" It
may perhaps be interesting to some to see the
sketch. It is as follows.

INTRODUCTION.

"My Friends,—You are now married. You
naturally look forward. You have entered
bonds, have entered for happiness, prompted by
natural feelings. You look around and see
misery in all classes. Some happy ones. You
ask why so much misery and so little happiness.
This is want of christian principles, feelings
and character. I wish to point out the most
common causes of domestic misery, and the
proper sources of domestic happiness.

Erroneous views of love. What is true love?
how to be encouraged and cultivated. Erroneous views of Friendship. What is Christian
friendship, and how to be cultivated. Erroneous expectations of each other — know not each
other fully during courtship, though disguise
be not intended. How to avoid this. Erroneous expectations of the duties of married life.
Enter it with thoughtlessness, when pressed
with its duties inclined to fly; should, on the
contrary, remain in the place of duty and rise
equal to the emergency. Confidence and jeal-

ousy. Erroneous views of rights — husband
wants to rule himself and wife — wife wants to
rule the husband;- constant bickerings, both are
equal. Differences of opinion on various mat--
ters— not expected people to have, in all things,
the same minds—must agree to differ. Religious differences. Intemperance, how brought
on — have nothing in the house. Personal and
domestic neatness — some are slovenly — house
always a dirt hole — avoid all this, women
should be neat in person, neat in everything.
Excessive worldliness. Some try to get all the
world — never find time to be happy — enjoy as
you go along. Extravagance. Fretfulness.
Scolding. Fashion. Good family management.
Domestics. Expecting to be *made* happy, by
outward circumstances. Want of mental occupation. Want of religious principles and hopes.
Expect attentions. Bad dispositions. Dissimi-
lar tastes. Unpleasant manners. Conclusion.

4. There appears also among his papers a
sketch of a volume entitled " Letters to a Friend
in Sickness," which may be interesting to some.
It is as follows : You are sick — you feel anxious to know how the event will terminate.
This is not the point of most importance. This
depends on a higher power. Endeavor to make
your mind easy. All will right. But your duty

to wish to live so long as you can be useful —
made for usefulness in this world. Selfish to
wish to die — no proof of piety. The convicts
and heathen often despise death. Even our
Saviour prayed for life. Try all means to
recover — observe all medical prescriptions.
Pray, but in imitation of Jesus — not your will,
but the will of God. How to regard sickness.
Dispensation of Providence — brought about by
natural causes. Father permitted such an
event. Duties of sickness, patience, obedience,
meekness, resignation, cheerfulness. Employment of time and thoughts. Settle at once all
your affairs of importance for this world, and
then banish them as much as possible from your
thoughts — that is, all merely worldly concerns;
all thoughts connected with education, morals,
religion and the like retain and cherish. Reading, such as what — New Testament. Meditation upon what subjects — Prayer. Views of
death. Death itself not to be feared — why?
Insanity — leaving relations — either poor, or
helpless or afflicted — all these immaterial—how
prepare for death. Seek correct views of yourself — of your Saviour — of your God — of
judgment and the punishment of sin. Immortality — certainty of it, from reason and revelation. Continued existence. Reason and Scrip-

ture. Know each other. Heaven — a state.
Qualifications for heaven, what—do you possess
them ? Improvement of sickness in case of recovery. Last moments, departure.

5. There appears among Mr Whitman's papers a sketch of the subjects merely of a volume to be entitled " Letters to the afflicted under
the loss of friends." The subjects are these,
What is resignation ? How to become resigned.
The death of Infants — of youth and middle-
aged. Old age — death of the profligate — of
the good.

6. There is still further a sketch of a plan of
a volume of letters "From a Father to his
Daughter," who had left home to work in a
Factory. It is as follows : " My dear daughter,
You are now about to leave the paternal roof.
Here we have enjoyed the sweets of domestic
life. I wish to give advice. I have worked in
this business myself. I know all about the busi-
ness in the mill — and the advantages out.
I wish to offer suggestions. Employment, hon-
orable, respectable. Use of money — you go
for the purpose of earning and acquiring some-
thing. Pedlers — charitable objects — dress.
Mourning apparel — ornaments. Improvement
—I have given you a good common education.
Still great room for improvement. Labor under

disadvantages — tired. But still something can be done — and I must regulate my advice by what I know can be accomplished. Improve every scrap of time. Attend Lyceum Lectures, you there pick up a great deal of knowledge. Reading every evening some one. Take such books as all can like. I know difficult, but persevere — talk about the things until you can bring them to it. Meditation — your employment favorable. Health — diet — sleeping apartment. Quack medicines to be avoided — clothing in all weathers. Exposure to wet — evening air — late at night — tight lacing — cleanliness — eating fruits, chalk and charcoal. India Rubbers — umbrellas — cloak — no beauty without health. Exercise. Religion — depend on yourself in regard to opinions. No one can answer for you ; decide for yourself. If only a good Christian, no matter what name. Go to meeting, never fail, many afraid to wear old dress. Have independence enough to do right. Choose your own meeting — you will be atacked. Mind none of these things. Hear for yourself. If I had a right to control you I should not dare to exercise it, because I cannot answer for you. You are the best judge. Read religious books — New Testament especially — other books, Sunday school lectures. Secret

devotion. Faithful to employers — abstain from
all evil — pursue *all* good. Happiness — you
wish to be happy — for this you were made. It
depends much on yourself. I will lay down a
few simple hints. Never do anything wrong,
you cannot be happy — always be improving.
You cannot look back with satisfaction upon
mere idleness, or innocence from actual sin.
Contentment — many are always thinking of
home, always talking of what they have left
behind and thus keep themselves in torment.
All these remembrances I wish you to leave.
Jealous — think neglected; selfish not willing
to do for others — be benevolent — fault-finding.
I have known many find fault with boarding
house. When you get a good boarding house
stick to it, put up with some inconveniences;
but fault-finding does no good, only increases
your unhappiness. Cheerfulness — confidence
in your Heavenly Father. Associates — you
must and will have associates. Associate freely
with all respectable persons. But you will have
some intimate friends of your own sex, and
some acquaintances of ours. I will, therefore,
give my advice on this topic. Choose those for
companions who are of amiable dispositions,
good principles and character — those too of
superior acquirements, so as to get good from

their acquaintance. In regard to young men
be civil to everybody ; have no acquaintance
with dissipated or unprincipled young men — no
good — but great injury will result from such an
acquaintance — look especially for correctness
of principles and character ; no matter about
polish or beauty. Many are anxious to have a
beau, indulge no feelings of this kind. Should
any proper person make advances and you become engaged — do nothing inconsistent with
your own self-respect. I have said these things
for your good, study them, obey them. You are
now separated from home, but do what is right
and we shall meet above to be no more separated."

Such are some of the sketches and plans for
future efforts found on loose scraps among his
papers. They evince a mind ever alive to the
wants of the community, and a fertility of in-
vention in preparing to meet these wants.
They shew a mind ever on the alert ; ever observing with a philosophic and religious eye
the condition of those around. A regard for
Mr Whitman's literary reputation would urge
the suppression of such hasty sketches. But
it is the object of biography to introduce the
readers to an acquaintance with its subjects. It
has been the object of this notice to introduce

its readers to an acquaintance with Mr Whitman just as he was; to enable them to look into his mind and heart, that they may see what was his character, what his aims and purposes and plans; to enable them to enter his study and see how incessantly he was thinking of and planning and laboring for the highest and best good of his race. Therefore these sketches, imperfect as they are, are given.

It is often the case that one, who is laboring with success for the community, and who is therefore held in high estimation by the mass, dwindles into insignificance, or manifests some strange peculiarities, when brought into contact with those of his own character and standing and profession. We naturally inquire, after these general accounts, what was the estimation in which Mr Whitman was held and the influence which he exerted among his ministering brethren. The character of Mr Whitman in this respect may be learned from the following letter written by one who was a member of the Clerical Association, to which Mr Whitman belonged. He writes thus: " With regard to your brother's influence among the brethren in the ministry and his character as a member of our Association, I am happy to state my impressions, for they are all such as I recall with

16*

u'nmingled pleasure. I am confident there was
not one of our Association, who did not love
and honor him. We never met him but with
greetings of the heart as well as of the hand.
His deportment among us was always marked
by the most childlike openness and simplicity
of manner and by a desire to impart and get
good. He was uniformly cheerful, frank and
hearty in his feeling and expressions. There
was no coldness about him to be warmed, no
suspicious disposition to be obviated, before we
could hold pleasant intercourse with him. We
felt at once that we were with a brother and a
friend — with one whose Christianity was to
him a well-spring of happy thoughts and generous affections. On all subjects that were discussed in our Association, he was accustomed
to express his views with great readiness and
precision. His inquisitive and thoughtful habit
of mind had led him to form pretty decided
opinions on all the important topics of religious
and social interest. He was never at a loss for
something to say that interested and enlightened
us. This arose not from a love of obtruding
himself, for no man had less of this fault, but
from the pleasure he took in communicating
thought, that he might receive thought in return.
His mind was a busy, free, ever working one,

and, among his brethren, its operations were ever observed with deep interest. His opinions, on the points that came before us, were received with great respect, and I believe there was no one of us, who did not think better of his own opinion upon finding that it agreed with Mr Whitman's. But the great charm of the intercourse we had with Mr Whitman was in the singleness of heart with which he aimed at the interests of truth and righteousness. Some persons may have been led into the mistaken idea that he was a mere party man in religious matters. Not so his brethren who knew him well and saw him much. They knew indeed that he was, as every Christian ought to be, attached to the theological views, which he had adopted, after patient investigation, and careful and devout estimate of evidences. But he loved his opinions, not because they were his, nor because they were those of his party; but because he believed them to be vitally connected with the interests of the Redeemer's kingdom. He doubtless had a strong love of religious discussion, but it was because he had a stronger love of the practical results, to which such discussions ought to lead in the establish-ment of christian faith and holiness. His polemical tendencies, whatever some may think,

were always subordinate to the interest he took
in the truth as it is in Jesus. Of this his
brethren had constant reason to be convinced,
for his mind was looking that way whatever
subject he discussed or whatever arguments
he advanced. I remember being particularly
struck with this, in the very interesting account
he gave us of his observations in the West after
his return from that region. A man, so popular and successful as he was on that visit, had
great temptation to indulge in the feelings of
partizanship. But he spoke of the importance
of diffusing Unitarianism in the West, and of
his desire to have it diffused there, solely as an
instrument of religious influence, not as a con-
quest to ' the cause,' but as an antagonist power
to infidelity and corruption, as a great and efficient aid to the progress of spiritual life in that
region, into which such miscellaneous multitudes
are pouring. In all that we saw or heard in
our intercourse with Mr Whitman, we found
him remarkably free from asperity and prejn-
dice. I never knew a man, who seemed to me
to have a better temper, and this is not common
place praise when said of one who engaged in
controversy so much as he did. He had a very
happy way of illustrating a subject, which came
up, by pleasant anecdotes or by familiar cases

which had fallen within his own observation, and the spirit in which he sketched these, was indicative of the most kindly feelings, while they sometimes threw a stronger light on the point than more labored illustrations. I believe, in short, that Mr Whitman's influence, in our Association and among his brethren generally, was of the happiest and best kind. And it was a strong influence, for no one could be indifferent to him. We remember him as one whom we honored for his virtues, his piety, his devotedness to truth, his christian graces, his warm and enlightened faith. When he died we felt that one of the best of God's gifts had been withdrawn from us — for what better gift can we have, than the presence of a good man and a fervent, devoted Christian ? We felt that he had blessed us in his life and blessed us in his death, and I hope we are grateful that we were permitted to know him and to love him."

At the present time, when the connexion between Pastor and people is so easily dissolved, it may be interesting to know Mr Whitman's views and conduct in regard to his connexion with his parish. In July 30, 1829, Mr Whitman's house of worship was struck with lightning. It became, at once, a question, whether it would not be for the best that his society should unite with the other society of the same faith in the place.   His feeling upon this point may be learned from a confidential letter to a female friend, written soon after the burning of the house.   He says, " As for our meeting-house, no two persons in the place perhaps were less affected than E. and myself.   We have got beyond being troubled by these afflictions [re-ferring to the death of Mrs Whitman's father and sister which had formed the subject of the first part of the letter, as well as to the burning of the house,] which are ordered by a merciful Father in infinite love.   We have always held ourselves ready to leave if circumstances re-quired.   I think it will be best for the town, that I should leave in the spring.   Let the whole town build a large house and they can unite."   In accordance with these views, Mr Whitman stated to the people, that, on his own account he would not have them rebuild.   He was ready to absolve them from any contract they had made.   But would leave it entirely to them, and would have them consult for the best inter-ests of themselves and of the whole town, with-out regard to him.   His people would not in-dulge, for a moment, the thought of parting with him.   A new meeting-house was therefore erected and dedicated on the first of January, 1830.

In June, 1831, Mr Whitman received an invitation to become the Pastor of the Unitarian Society, in Cincinnati, Ohio. His own feelings would have prompted him to accept. He had become acquainted with the society and held it in very high estimation. He felt a deep interest in the spread of liberal views in the region. He regarded the field of labor and of usefulness as one of the most important and extensive and one well calculated for his peculiar talents But he had a sacred regard for duty and asked only what that might require. He had a tender regard for the feelings of his people and for their religious welfare. The letter containing the invitation was addressed to the people and he made known to them his willingness to be governed by their decision. They voted, *unanimously*, not to part with him, and to manifest still further their regard and attachment to him, and their wish to have him regard Waltham as his *home*, they, at the same meeting, appointed a committee to procure subscriptions to aid in building him a dwelling-house.

In October, 1833, Mr Whitman was appointed General Secretary of the American Unitarian Association. This appointment accorded well with his feelings, with his earnest missionary zeal. It seemed to open a field of useful

ness of almost boundless extent, and one for
which he might suppose himself, if he judged
by the unanimity with which he was chosen,
somewhat adapted. The support offered was
much greater than what he was receiving from
his parish, and he knew too, from his past experience and success in labors somewhat similar, especially in the Valley of the West, that he
might expect those striking visible results which
are so gratifying. There seemed then to be
every reason why he should accept. And to all
general and obvious reasons, it may be added,
that his own feelings strongly prompted him to
accept. But here, as before, a regard for duty,
for the feelings and the welfare of his people
triumphed over all general reasons and all inward promptings. He referred the committee
of the American Unitarian Association, appointed to communicate with him upon the subject, to his people for their answer. And,
although he signified his willingness to accept
could their consent be gained, he also expressed
his determination to abide by their decision.
Application was made to his people. But they
voted again, *unanimously*, not to part with him,
thus affording another proof of the strong hold
he had secured upon their affections.

Mr Whitman was not an unconcerned spec-

tator of the various movements of his day.
He looked upon them all with deep interest,
and, after examination, he formed decided opinions in regard to them, which he was ever ready
to express and defend. The Anti-masonic
movement was exciting much interest in the
community. Mr Whitman was a mason. He
was not a zealous and enthusiastic mason. But
he had joined the Lodge and had taken some
degrees. And he could see no reason why he
should renounce his masonry. He felt that the
Institution had been abused. But he felt too
that many of the charges of Anti-masons were
unfounded, the spirit manifested and the course
pursued by them improper ; he suspected the
motives by which many of their leaders were influenced. He was not one, that would shrink
from standing forth in defence of what he regarded as an abused institution. He did therefore, at the dedication of the Masonic Temple,
in Boston, and on other occasions, stand forth
in defence of Masonry.

The Anti-slavery movement had begun to excite deep interest. Mr Whitman looked at the
subject with calmness and with candor. He
availed himself of every opportunity to gain correct information. When he visited the South,
— slave-holding States, — his eyes were open.

17

While at the same time he reflected much and
deeply upon the abstract principles of right and
wrong as applicable to the case.   For a time he
hesitated to express a decided opinion upon the
subject.   He was deliberating.   But at length
some time during the year previous to his death,
he took an open and decided stand upon Anti-
slavery ground.   He disapproved of many of the
measures of the most violent of the party.   But he
once said to the writer, " the principles upon
which this movement is based are the eternal
principles of rectitude.   Shall we refrain from
taking an open stand in favor of truth and righteousness, through fear of opposition, or from
disgust at the measures of the friends of truth ?
I believe the Gospel to be the truth of God.
Shall I hesitate to take an open stand in favor
of the Gospel, through fear of opposition or because I have been disgusted, as I most certainly
have been, with many of the measures of the
friends of the Gospel ?   No.   This cause is the
cause of truth, of right, of God.   It must, it
will prevail.   It becomes me and all who are
satisfied upon the subject to exert our influence
as far as we may to prevent that wild excess of
over zealous enthusiasts, which may ruin the
best of causes."   He watched carefully the opposition to this cause which was excited, and

regarded it all as permitted by God in wisdom, and had faith to believe that it would all be overruled for the advancement of truth and righteousness. He did not feel himself called to leave the regular duties of his profession and engage in labors to advance this cause. But he was ever ready, after having made up his mind, to speak in its favor in public as well as in private.

The Temperance movement was another subject of deep and exciting interest. Upon this subject Mr Whitman deliberated as he had done in regard to Anti-slavery. He, from the first, acknowledged the evils, but had doubts in regard to the remedies. He weighed every point carefully before he decided. Upon one occasion, the writer was advocating the expediency, propriety and importance of the pledge, when Mr Whitman took opposite ground and expressed his doubts and objections. But shortly after, convinced by his own reflections upon the subject, he took open and decided ground in favor of the pledge. At one time, he doubted the expediency of abstinence from wine. But, convinced by his own reflections upon the subject, he discontinued himself the practice of offering it to visitors, or of using it himself. He did not publicly advocate the extending of the pledge to include wine, but he did publicly. express his opinion and make known his own practice upon the subject. The advancement of this cause he considered as so important, and so vitally connected with the prosperity of the church, the best interests of pure and undefiled religion, that he regarded it but as a part of his duty to labor earnestly and zealously in it. He therefore devoted to it, for a time, the whole energies of his system. He prepared himself to speak, to lecture upon the subject. And an anecdote may shew that he took hold of the subject with his whole heart. He told the writer, in speaking upon the subject, that he had spent the night in dreams upon it, and in his dreams had studied out what he believed must be a convincing and satisfactory argument. He went forth then to labor in this cause with all the zeal of his naturally ardent temperament, and devoted to it the whole strength of his intellect. He labored not only with earnestness but with success. He became at once a popular Temperance Lecturer. He was sent for in all directions and by the members of various religious denominations. His popularity was not secured by the relation of anecdotes, the exciting a laugh and affording amusement; but by the clear, direct and conclusive reasoning presented, and by the circumstance, that, while he spoke plainly and earnestly upon the subject, he also spoke in the most perfect kindness. Says a friend in writing upon this subject, "He used, in his Temperance addresses, to take the bull by the horns. He would place himself behind the counter or within the bar, and imagine the train of thought passing in the retailer's mind. He would shew the fallacy of the reasoning — would demolish it by his powerful arguments, and then would appeal to the retailer himself, with the utmost kindness and good temper and ask if he were mistaken in what he had imagined. If it was not as he had said, he professed himself willing to take back his statements. But, if the correctness of his statements was admitted, he urged home, with the greatest possible plainness and point, the practical application of them. And, what was remarkable, he did all this in such a manner as not to give offence to the individuals so directly addressed.

Early in the spring of 1834, Mr Whitman delivered a Temperance Address at the Seamen's Chapel, Boston (Rev. Mr Taylor's). Upon exposing himself to the evening air after speaking, he caught a very severe cold. He was much troubled with hoarseness and a severe

cough. But he had ever regarded himself as
constitutionally secured against the danger of
consumptive complaints. He was not therefore
particularly anxious in regard to the result of
his cough, nor particularly careful to avoid exposure or to refrain from the exercise of his
lungs in public speaking. He performed, for a
time, his usual duties upon the Sabbath, and
held himself ready to speak at other times
upon the subject of Temperance. Upon being
cautioned by a friend in regard to his course,
and reminded that his cough in this way might
become fixed and prove fatal — he threw open
his coat and said, "did you ever know a man
with such a chest die of consumption ?"

Some time about the last of April or the beginning of May, 1834, Mr Whitman visited his
father at East Bridgewater, and spent the Sabbath there. It was his intention to preach for
Rev. Mr Crafts during a part of the day, and
deliver a Temperance Address in the evening.
But, when the time arrived, he did not feel himself able to preach during any part of the day.
He did however make an effort and deliver his
Temperance Address in the evening. This
was his native place. Some of his school mates
had been ruined by intemperance. His feelings
were deeply interested. He spoke with great

earnestness, for nearly two hours, although so
hoarse before he finished, that it was painful to
hear him.   He never afterwards spoke in public.

Upon his return to Waltham, he discontinued,
at the suggestion of his Physician, his pulpit
labors and indeed all efforts of every kind which
might interfere with his devotion to his health.
His cough remained, and other symptoms seemed alarming.   In the early part of the summer
it was suggested that perhaps relief might be
obtained by journeying.   He therefore started
in company with Mrs Whitman and a brother,
and by short and easy stages went as far as
Belchertown, Mass., where his eldest brother
Captain James Whitman resided.   But he found
himself as he thought losing instead of gaining
strength by his journey, and he turned back
again.   He spent a few days at the springs in
Hopkinton, Mass., and then returned to Waltham, believing, as he said, that *home* was the
best place for the sick.   The effects of this
short journey satisfied Mr Whitman that he was
laboring under a seated, confirmed consumption,
from which there was no hope of escape.   He
felt that his days were numbered, and that he
was called upon to apply his principles to a new
class of temptations and duties.   As he once
said to the writer, " I have, ever since my jour-

ney, been fully satisfied in regard to myself. I have not indeed expressed my feelings, for I would not cut short the hopes indulged by my friends and by which they are sustained, and I have felt it to be my duty to obey every prescription of my physician, and to do all in my power to secure, if possible, a restoration to health. But I am not disappointed at the result, for I have been fully satisfied, from the time of my journey, of my real condition." He now put in practice, at once, the hints contained in his sketched plan of "Letters to the Sick." He endeavored to settle up as far as was in his power all his worldly matters, his affairs of mere business, or give such information and directions as would assist others in arranging them. The writer was called upon to assist in this, and often was he in the sick room for the mere transaction of business, about which Mr Whitman would set himself with as much calmness as he had ever in his life done. For a time, while it was thought there might still be hope, he was careful to avoid all company which might fatigue and injure him. The Rev. Mr Ripley was almost the only person, besides the members of the family, who was at this time allowed free access at all times to his chamber. With this gentleman Mr Whitman had for nearly ten years been associated on terms of the most perfect and uninterrupted peace and har-mony, of the most unreserved freedom and intimacy. The houses of each were ever open to the other as a member of the family. But, as Mr Whitman became enfeebled by disease, he naturally clung to those around him with a stronger and more yearning affection than when in full strength he felt a greater degree of dependence upon himself. He was ever glad to see Mr Ripley enter his room — enjoyed much in conversation with him, and often, during his absence, spoke with manifestations of the deepest feelings of gratitude, of the kindness and attention and sympathy which he had experienced at the hands of this christian brother. Indeed Mr Whitman often spoke with deep gratitude of the many kind attentions which he was every day receiving from all his friends.

When the Physicians themselves had pronounced his case hopeless, he altered his course in regard to company and saw most of those, especially of his brethren in the ministry, who called at proper hours. He requested the writer to say to his brethren in Boston, that he would not have them stay away out of regard to his weakness, for it would give him pleasure to see them. When one who had visited him was taking his leave and apologized, saying that perhaps by his conversation he had wearied him and should wear him out; Mr Whitman, with a pleasant smile, said, "*I must wear out*, and it is pleasant to see and converse with my friends, while the process is going on." When his friends called to see him they found him cheerful and happy; perfectly aware of his situation, watching, with all the care and all the calmness of a physician, the various successive symptoms of his disease as they indicated the nearer approach of dissolution, and ever ready to converse upon his departure, his hopes for the future world, and his views and feelings in the full and near prospect of death. Said one who had visited him to the writer, " My feelings, as I approached the house, were of the most melancholy character. The thought that one so active, one so extensively useful, one of so much promise in regard to future efforts, should he thus cut down in the midst of his years and strength, this thought filled me, as I drew near to the house, with feelings of the deepest melancholy. But the moment I entered the room my feelings changed; the peaceful and happy expression of countenance exhibited by the emaciated sufferer, the cheerfulness of his conversation, not a light and trifling cheer-

fulness, but a sobered cheerfulness, arising from
pure feelings within, from a holy confidence in
his heavenly Father, and from a bright view of
happy prospects before him, all served to banish
feelings of melancholy, and to brighten up
the scene with a beam as it were from the eternal world."

Mr Whitman enjoyed much pleasure in see-
ing his friends. As he assured the writer, with
but a single exception, he had been *relieved* by
their visits. And, in regard to this exception,
he discovered, he said, after a time, that the
individual was troubled with a nervous and
trembling dread of death. "When I discovered this," he said, "I spoke upon the subject
as well as I was able, in hopes, that, if what I
said was feeble, the *pulpit* from which I was
preaching might give it weight." Thus true
was he to the great principle of his life, availing himself of every casual interview with a
friend to do him good.

Mr Whitman undoubtedly suffered much
pain. But so careful was he of the feelings of
others, and so anxious to avoid giving unneces-
sary trouble, that he seldom spoke of the pain
and suffering he endured. He spent much of
his time in reading and hearing reading. The
New Testament was his principal book. Other

books of a practical character, together with
devotional poetry, afforded him much pleasure
He also read the newspapers and kept up his
interest in the affairs of the community, especially in regard to its religious condition. He
dwelt much, in his conversations with the writer,
upon the importance of plain, simple, earnest
preaching. "It is not," said he, "it is not to
give information, it is to awaken attention that
we preach. Go through our parishes, and what
do we want? an earnest, plain and direct mode
of preaching."

Such was the appearance of Mr Whitman,
during his sickness. With the event of death
directly before him, distinctly in view, satisfied
himself that there was no possibility of escape,
and perceiving by the changing symptoms of
his disease, that he was gradually drawing
nearer and nearer to that event; he was ever
cheerful and calm and happy. With his eye
fixed upon the eternal world he did not forget
this; but cherished his interest in his friends;
his interest in the prospects of religion; his
interest in the best welfare of the community.
Upon the very verge of spiritual existence, he
did not forget that his own spiritual improvement was to be carried out and perfected by the
right discharge of the duties of sickness. He

spent much thought upon his past course, much
time in self-examination. He examined again his
religious opinions. He felt confirmed, from his
self-examination, that he had done what was important at the time in his controversial writings.
He felt more and more fully satisfied with his
own pure, simple and rational faith. He had
in health, and before the public, argued its
scriptural foundation ; he had in the trying
scenes of life manifested its controlling influence ; he was ready, upon what he himself regarded as his own death bed, to bear testimony
to its sustaining power. He had valued his own
peculiar views in health, not because they were
his, but because he felt them to be the power of
God to Salvation. He clung to them in death,
for he found in them all tho support which he
needed.

Mr Whitman continued to waste gradually
away. He rode out till within a few weeks
previous to his death. On the morning of the
5th of Nov. he said that " he found a difficulty
in awaking," and asked " if anything had been
given him to make him sleep." He was assured
there had not. He asked " if the room was
not darker than usual." He was assured that
it was not. He said, " is not my mind awake ?"
He then said that he was dying, and, as there

was no man in the house, requested that his
brother, Mr Hosea Whitman, who lived near
should be sent for. He was asked if he would
have the physician called. He said, "as a
friend I shou'd be glad to see him — he can do
me no good." After 'some moments he said,
" *Father, receive my spirit — I die in peace with
all.*" In a short time he added, " *my firm faith
in Christ supports me now.*" These were his
last words. The physician, as he had previously
expressed a desire to be present if possible at
this scene, was called. Mr Whitman lay for
some time, perfectly sensible, as was shewn by
his extending his hand when the physician from
time to time approached the bed, until at length
with scarcely a struggle he fell asleep.

So lived, and so died the Rev. Bernard Whitman. And now the melancholy task which
nought but a sense of duty would have induced
me to enter upon, and which has been much
delayed by circumstances beyond my control, is
brought to a close. If I have succeeded in
laying open the mind and heart of the subject
of my notice to my readers, there is no need of
any general summary, from me. If I have not,
all that I could add, would be of no avail. If
what I have written shall awaken a single one

to the value of our pure and simple faith, and
the importance of a life of devotion to truth and
duty, I shall feel that my labors have been
rewarded. Nay more, I shall cherish the feeling that the spirit, whose earthly course of trial
and duty and improvement I have endeavored to
describe, will, even in the regions of heavenly
blessedness, rejoice over such a result.

It is believed that this Memoir would be imperfect without the Address of Rev. Mr Ripley
at the funeral of Mr Whitman, and that it can
not be more appropriately closed than by the
insertion of that interesting notice of his last
days.

ADDRESS.

The melancholy occasion on which we are here
assembled, my friends, demands more than ordinary notice ; for he, whose death we lament, was
an extraordinary man. He filled and nobly sustained a wider field of action than most men. He
marked out and executed great and important plans,
which had relation to, and influence upon, the
highest interests of human beings, for time and for
eternity. Most important and interesting associations were connected with his life, — and his
death has left a void in society, in the intellectual
and moral relations of active life, which cannot, I
fear, be so well filled by any other person.

But, my friends, I have not come here to portray
to you the character of your late beloved pastor ; —
for you are all familiar with it ;— nor to make
known to you his religious sentiments and the vast
energies of his ever active mind and benevolent
soul ;— for these have long been known to ,you in
his preaching, his labors by night and day, in the
cause of truth and virtue. And his religoius opinions, and the zeal with which he maintained them,
are before the world in his published writings and
discourses. No. I come not here to eulogize him,
whose best eulogy was his whole life and conversation in the world, which you have seen, and
heard, and felt. My object now is, to give some
striking proofs of his deep, heart-felt piety, manifested through his long sickness, and at the hour of
death. To show you, that he was supported by,
and died in the faith, by which he had lived. And
in doing this, I fulfil the request of our friend, made
to me a few days before his death. You will
therfore receive what I tell you as coming from
him. " Though dead, you will hear him yet
speaking to you " of his strong and unchanged convictions of religious truth and duty, his high and
holy hope, his unfeigned humility, and meek submission, his support and consolations, his bright,
heavenly anticipations.

In one of my visits to him not a fortnight before
his death, I found him calm and composed, as
usual, and disposed to converse freely. I said to
him, it has always been my hope that you would

evince in your sickness, the power, the supporting
power of the religious sentiments you have so con-
sistently maintained ; and I am rejoiced to find my
expectations realized. He replied, " my religious
sentiments are the same now, that they were in
health ; the same I have always preached and
maintained. I feel the need of no other. I find
them able to support and comfort me, and they
have never failed to console me. I believe farther,
that they are a sufficient support for the Christian,
in life and in death. I have asked myself seriously,
if I required any other support ; if the belief of
any other sentiments or doctrines were necessary
to me. I examined the other day the Calvinistic
doctrines, and tried to apply them to myself, to see
if they could give me any more consolation or support, but I tried in vain. I could find no room for
them, no need of them, no consolation in them, nor
could I find them in the Bible — Few and simple,"
said he, " are the essential articles of my belief;
belief in God as my Father and Friend, in his paternal and overruling providence ; in Jesus Christ,
as the all-sufficient Saviour and Redeemer ; in the
resurrection of the soul to eternal life ; in a future
retribution of rewards and punishments, according
to the conduct and character of the present life.
My faith in the immortality of man is strong and
cheering. And I believe that it commences with
his departure from this world ;— that the soul goes
from this life to judgment, in the presence of God.
I believe man was made for happiness here and

forever, and that Jesus Christ was sent upon earth
to teach men by his religion and example, his life
and death, how to gain this happiness ;— that to
be happy we must be good, and we can be good
only by the influence of religious principles.   I believe all is right, that God appoints.   As for myself, I have not now, nor have I had during my
sickness one moment's anxiety.   I submit entirely
to my physician and to the Almighty.   Whatever
they direct, I shall cheerfully do, and submit to."
I observed to him, that although he was taken
from his labors so early in life, in the midst of his
plans of usefulness, still he had great cause of
thankfulness to God, that he had been enabled to
accomplish so much, in a short time ; so much
more than most of us effected in a long ministry.
He replied, "I am thankful ; and I could have
wished, had it been God's will, to have lived to do
much more ; for I had marked out much work
which I intended to execute.   I had prepared
skeletons of a course of sermons, principally for
the young, which I had hoped to fill out and preach
this summer ; and determined upon my plan of
labors for some time to come.   But God has ordered otherwise, and I bow to his will."   I reminded
him of the last discourse, which he preached to my
people, a few weeks before he was confined by
sickness, and which seemed to make a deep impression on all who heard it.   "Yes," said he, "that
is the best method of enforcing moral and religious
truth, by apt and familiar illustrations, brought

home to every soul. Had I lived I should have preached more than ever, in that way, — the only way in which preaching, as it seems to me, can do much good. Indeed, said he, I had just begun to learn how to preach. I should not in future, have devoted much attention to controversy, because the time has gone by, when I think it was needed. My preaching would be for the most part, practical ; illustrating the paternal character of God, the life and example of Christ, the importance of early religoius education. That," said he, with emphasis, " is the *grand point*, that is the foundation of a religious character. I do not mean to say, that I regret having been engaged in religious controversy. And though some things which I wrote, and some expressions which I used, may have seemed harsh and severe, I thought them necessary at the time, and that I was doing my duty to truth and religion. And I do not now regret the course I pursued." A few days after this conversation, I visited our friend again. I found him more feeble in body but strong and bright in intellect, humble and resigned in spirit. He had expected my visit, and at once entered upon the most interesting of subjects, about which few are able to speak with calmness, when they feel that the events of which they speak are soon to be realized, and the duties they suggest soon to be executed. I refer to this occasion, these solemnities, and the manner in which they should be performed. At this time he spake most feelingly of the kindness and attention of his friends, and

the people of his parish, generally ; of the kindness of many out of his parish, on whom he had
no claims, but the claims of humanity and Christian
sympathy. He often talked to me of his people —
how grateful he felt for their kindness, and solic-
itude for him ; how happy his situation was in
sickness compared with many others ; that every
want was supplied ; every desire was gratified,
even anticipated. And I can assure you, my friends,
that it would have afforded him the purest satisfaction to have seen you, and talked with you often,
had it been consistent with a prudent care of himself, and the endeavors used to restore him to
health and usefulness. But after his return from
his journey, and before his disease was decided to
be incurable, it was absolutely necessary that he
should be kept free from all excitement, and when
all hope of recovery had left him, physical inabil-
ity rendered it inpossible for him to endure much
company. But he did not forget you, even to the
last. His chief concern was for you, your present,
your eternal welfare. The last time I saw your
pastor was the afternoon before his death ; a day
ever to be remembered by me. As I entered his
chamber a scene presented itself, which made an
impression on my mind, that will never be effaced.
There was just light enough in the room, to enable
his friend, who sat by his side, to read to him devotional hymns, and those beautiful and sublime
chapters, the 14th and 17th of John and the 15th
of Corinthians. The calm and serene and holy

expression of his countenance, — the bright and heavenly lustre of his eyes, — all spoke with an eloquence which language cannot describe of peace and heaven within. I felt the place to be holy. I said to him, you are highly favored, my brother, in being so free from suffering, that you can indulge these meditations, and pass your hours in these exercises, which will shortly form your employment and delight forever. Your heaven has already commenced. "Yes," said he, "I have indeed a foretaste of heaven; I have communion with heavenly spirits. Some of my dreams have been most delightful. When I leave my friends on earth, I shall only go to a larger family in heaven. If I had strength, I could talk ; I could preach to those around me. I could pray and tell of my experiences. But I dislike all display. One short line expresses all I feel and wish to say. 'Father, thy will be done.' That is enough."

"Is this his death bed ? No — it is his shrine;
Behold him there, just rising to a God.
The chamber where the good man meets his fate
Is priveleged beyond the common walk
Of virtuous life, quite in the verge of heaven."

In giving this relation of the religious sentiments and feelings of your late pastor, his grateful and affectionate feelings towards you, his deep concern for your spiritual welfare, I have done as he requested, and as nearly as I could, I have given you his own words. And do you not perceive the perfect consistency of his character. In everything he has done do you not see the *man* as he was, the *Christian* as he should be? I love to dwell on his character — his Christian character. Never have I seen more completely exemplified the power of religous faith to sustain, cheer and console the Christian, than in him, during the whole of his sickness. Never have I witnessed such childlike submission to the will of God. The last moments of his life are confirmation of this ; for when he perceived himself to be dying, he said, " O Father, receive my spirit. I die in peace with all." After a pause he added, "my firm faith in Christ supports me now." Who could witness such a scene and not exclaim, " Let me die the death of the righteous, and my last end be like his!" In this humble yet exalted and heavenly frame of mind, our friend closed his present being. And will it henceforth be said that the simple truths of the Gospel, as we believe them, are not adequate to support the Christian in life and in death ; that they cannot prepare him for the eternal world? Has he not passed into the eternal world, resting on this faith, in the firm belief of these religious sentiments? Consoled, supported and animated by these, he has gone to his Father and our Father, and commenced a wider and higher scene of duty and enjoyment, in the world of pure and perfected spirits.

And now, my friends, though these walls will no more echo to the voice of him, whom you delighted to hear ; though that voice will no more be raised

to quicken your faith and call you to duty; he still
lives.   He lives not only to God, and to the spirits
of the just made perfect in Hea,ven, but he lives to
you.   He lives to you in every good principle,
which he nurtured in your souls, in every pious
and benevolent impression he has made upon your
hearts.   Though dead he yet speaketh to,yon, as it
were from the other world, in language more powerful than any he ever addressed to you on carth.
The example of his active and benevolent life is
fresh in your minds, and you will never forget the
brighter example of his faith, humility and resignation in sickness and death.   In all these, he speaks,
he exhorts, he encourages you.   The thought of
him will no doubt be associated with many a good
resolution, with many a holy wish, with many a
pious aspiration.   When your faith is tried by ridicule and scorn, you will remember how manfully
he defended it against his open and secret enemies,
and you will feel safe with the anchor on which he
rested.   When you are strongly tempted to take
the first dangerous step in the path that leads to
death, you will hear his warning voice and perhaps
forbear. Yes. The good can never die. The
veil of flesh cannot entirely separate them. They
form but one great family. Their home is with
God. Thither he has gone before you, and beck-
ons you onward to the same mansions of peace and
love and eternal joy.